10 WIRE AND CANVAS DECOY PATTERNS FOR CARVERS

Al Streetman

Schiffer Publishing Ltd

4880 Lower Valley Road, Atglen, PA 19310 USA

Library of Congress Catalog Card Number: 99-64845

Designed by "Sue"
Type set in Copperplate Gothic/Goudy OlSt

ISBN: 0-7643-0978-1
Printed in China

Published by Schiffer Publishing Ltd.
4880 Lower Valley Road
Atglen, PA 19310
Phone: (610) 593-1777; Fax: (610) 593-2002
Please visit out web site catalog at
www.schifferbooks.com or write for a free catalog.
This book may be purchased from the publisher.
Please include $3.95 for shipping.

In Europe, Schiffer books are distributed by
Bushwood Books
6 Marksbury Rd.
Kew Gardens
Surrey TW9 4JF England
Phone: 44 (0)181 392-8585; Fax: 44 (0)181 392-9876
E-mail: Bushwd@aol.com

Please try your bookstore first.

We are interested in hearing from authors
with book ideas on related subjects.

Contents

Introduction 5
General Notes 6
General Painting Suggestions 7
Constructing the Goose Body and Head 9
Covering the Body 25
Painting the Goose 33
Antiquing the Goose 35
The Gallery 37
Reference Section:
"T"-Holding rig for decoys 49
General Reference and Information Sheet 50
Sources of Supplies, Materials, and Catalogs 51
Gouge Reference Chart 52
Patterns 53

Acknowledgments

The following people helped make this book possible. I thank you all.
Gary Voorhies: Woodcrafters of Oklahoma, for your continued support.
Delta Technical Coatings: The paint samples were excellent, and satisfactory in all respects.
Woodcrafters of Oklahoma: High-quality carving tools and supplies.
Royal Brush Mfg., Inc.: Excellent quality paintbrushes at an affordable price.

Introduction

In response to numerous people who have seen my wire and canvas decoys (or others similar to them), and have asked me "How are they made?", this book is for you. Whether you are new to the art of decoy making, or an old hand at making wooden decoys and just looking for a new direction, I hope you find something of interest here.

Decoys of this type were popular around the Eastern shore area of Virginia and the Carolinas, near the turn of the 20th century. Because an abundance of good carving wood was not handy, decoy-makers in this region had to use ingenuity in order to create replicas of large birds such as the Canada Goose. Somehow, they figured out that a small amount of wood, combined with old wire and possibly one of their wives' old bed sheets, could be fashioned into a passable decoy that would get the job done.

An advantage of decoys fashioned in this manner was their light weight. This allowed many more to be carried by an individual, compared to the weight that a similar number of solid wood decoys would have. A disadvantage might have been the anger visited upon the decoy-maker when his wife discovered that her favorite bed linens were covering not her bed, but the ducks floating in the bay!

Except for the actual carving project, I have not included specific carving instructions. I have found that each carver has his or her own style, and each has their preference for which tool to use in a particular area, or to achieve a particular effect.

Rather than giving a vague instruction such as "use a small gouge", I have listed the particular sizes of gouges I used through each different step of the carving project. This is more for the benefit of the beginning carver, rather than the more experienced ones. If you don't have these particular sizes of gouges or tools, use something similar.

Because of space and page considerations, the patterns in this book have been reduced to 60% of their original size. As described on page 6, the patterns will need to be enlarged 166% to reach the size I designed them to be. If you desire a larger or smaller version, simply enlarge or shrink the pattern on a photocopying machine.

GENERAL NOTES

1. Trace the pattern you have decided to carve, or make a copy of it on a photocopying machine. Glue the pattern you copied or traced onto some heavy paper such as poster paper or a manila file folder. When the glue is dry, cut out the pattern. This method will prevent you from ruining the master patterns in your book.

2. Lay your pattern on the wood, trace the outline of it, and saw it out. **The arrows shown on the patterns, with a "G" superimposed over them, indicate the recommended grain direction of the wood to obtain best results and easiest carving.**

3. You should now have a rough blank ready to be carved.

4. Use your own techniques and style to bring the carving to the finished stage.

For those of you who are not familiar with the type of cuts different gouges make, or how large the cut is for a specific size of gouge, I have included a Gouge Reference Chart in this book. If you want to use a different gouge other than one which I used, this chart will be helpful in determining what type of gouge you might want to try.

5. For those of you who have never had much practice enlarging or reducing patterns, or being able to calculate how much enlargement or reduction you need to select on the photocopying machine, here are some general guidelines.

Let's say you have a pattern that shows a side profile requiring 2" thick wood, and you want to make the pattern larger so it will fit on 3" thick wood. Use the following formula to calculate what percentage enlargement to select on the copier:

[New Dimension Desired ÷ Present Dimension] x 100 = %

to select on copier machine. Using our example, this would work out as follows:

[3" ÷ 2"] x 100 = **150 %.**

Going the other way, let's say you have a pattern that shows a 2" side profile, and you want to reduce it down so it will fit on a piece of 1-3/4" thick wood. Using the same formula, it works out as follows:

[1.75" ÷ 2"] x 100 = **87.5 %.**

If the machine you are using won't go large enough or small enough to get the job done on the first try, additional steps may be required. Go ahead and make your first copy using the largest enlargement or reduction setting you can select. Measure the *new* dimensions on your *copy,* (which will now be your Present Dimension), then use the same formula as before to calculate how much additional enlargement or reduction is needed to get the pattern to the size you desire it to be.

6. I have found that no fancy or special wood is needed to construct decoys of this type. Regular pine shelving from any lumber source is fine for making the bottom and back sections. The only concession to fine wood I make is in the head. Here, I prefer to use Basswood or White Pine, simply because I want to be able to carve and detail the head without having to cut through knots and hard wood.

General Painting Suggestions For All Patterns In This Book

I have included some *suggested* colors for all patterns. If you have a preference for a different color scheme, by all means use it. If decoy painting is new to you, most local libraries have a multitude of books showing color schemes of the various waterfowl. Also, most bookstores have a large selection of duck and decoy books available for purchase. Study the pictures in the books, and paint your decoy to resemble it. Simple paint schemes, such as the one I used on the project in this book, are effective and easy to master. As your painting skills progress, you can make the decoy paint scheme as fancy as you wish. I purposely used a simple scheme in the book for two reasons: (1) This was based on an old decoy I made a sketch of for a reference, and (2) I didn't want to terrify beginners with a monstrously difficult paint job!

I have listed the colors produced by Delta Technical Coatings, Inc. and their identification numbers, which I have found to be suitable for painting the carving project, and all my other carvings. I have used these colors, and the results were excellent. I hope this will help minimize your confusion when trying to sort through the maze of paint brands and colors at your hobby or craft store. The best paintbrushes I have found, for the money, are made by the Royal Brush Mfg. Company. They come in a wide assortment of sizes and shapes, are durable, and (most important) are affordable. In general, here are the ones I use and recommend for painting your carvings.

- Royal Golden Taklon series 250 Round, size 0 and 00: Details such as eyes and other small areas.
- Royal Golden Taklon series 170 Cat's Tongue, size 2 and 4: Large areas.
- Royal Golden Taklon series 150 Short Shader, size 2 and 4: Blending colors. (For example, when blending a one color into another color, such as the bill of a Canvasback duck into the head area).

I have listed general color schemes, because decoys made in this style were not painted to be displayed in museums. They were painted just well enough to fool the intended goose or duck into gunning range. By the time an unsuspecting bird realized he (or she) had been "had", it was too late.

If you have had prior experience making and painting decoys, you are welcome and encouraged to add more detail in the painting. Add feather strokes, blend in more color shifts, or do whatever else you might feel is needed to get the decoy just the way you want it to look.

Canada Goose

Head and Tail Patch: Black #2506
Body, Front and Rear: White #2505
Body, Main Part: Territorial Beige #2425
Eyes: Dark Brown #2053 with Black pupil

Swan

Bill: Black #2506
Head, Neck and Body: White #2505
Lightly sponge or dry-brush over the White areas with Burnt Umber #2025
Eyes: Dark Brown #2053 with Black pupil

Canvasback

Bill: Black #2506
Head and Neck: Burnt Sienna #2030, then lightly dry-brush with Raw Sienna #2411
Body (Front of chest): Black #2506; Back and sides: White #2505, lightly dry-brushed over with Black #2506; Tail: Black #2506
Eyes: Cardinal Red # 2077, with Black Pupil

Redhead

Bill: Chambray Blue #2514 with Black tip
Head and Neck: Burnt Sienna #2030
Body (Front of chest): Burnt Umber #2025; Back and sides: White #2505, lightly dry-brushed over with Black #2506; Tail: Black #2506
Eyes: Opaque yellow #2509, with Black pupil

American Goldeneye

Bill: Black #2506
Head and Neck: Burnt Umber #2025
Body (Chest): White #2505; Sides and back: White #2505, then medium dry-brush with Burnt Umber #2025 and Black #2506
Eyes: Pale Yellow #2005

Bufflehead

Bill: White #2505, then medium dry-brushed over with Black #2506
Head and back (except for patch on head): Black #2506
Patch on head and body sides: White #2505
Eyes: Dark Brown #2053 with Black pupil

Hooded Merganser

Bill, main part of head, and upper surface of back: Black #2506
Patch on head and front part of chest: White #2505
Sides of body: Walnut #2024
Eyes: Opaque Yellow #2509

Mallard

Bill: Crocus Yellow #2459
Head: Mallard Green #2491
Chest: Burnt Sienna #2030
Neck Band and body sides: White #2505
Upper surfaces of back: Cadet Grey #2426
Tail area: Black #2506
Eyes: Dark Brown #2053 with Black pupil

Pintail

Bill: Black #2506
Head (main part): Brown Velvet #2109
Chest and stripe up sides of head: White #2505
Body: Drizzle Grey #2452 with light dry-brush over of Black
Tail: Black #2506
Eyes: Dark Brown #2053 with Black pupil

Constructing the Goose Body and Head

If you don't already have one from previous decoy-carving adventures, refer to the instructions in this book and construct a "T"-Holding rig from some scrap wood. We will need it shortly, so go ahead and get it made.

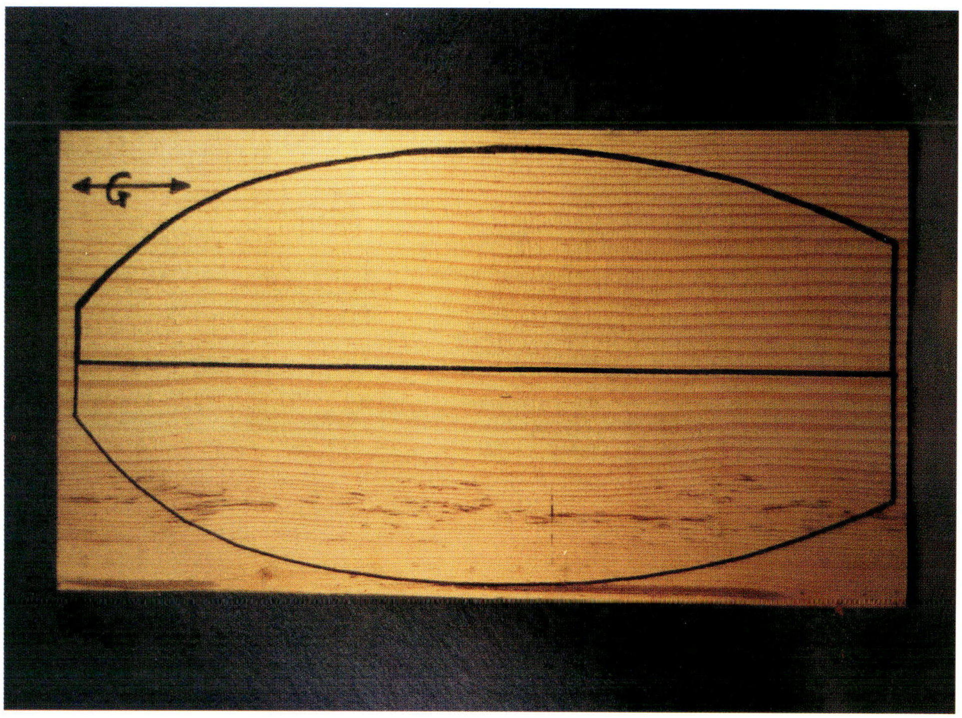

Transfer the outline of the goose bottom to a section of 3/4"-thick wood shelving. Multiply the widest part of the pattern by 2 to establish the width of wood you will need to make the bottom section from one piece. (Trace one-half of the bottom pattern, then flip it over and trace the other half). This will provide a full-size bottom section pattern, which we will saw out shortly.

Lay the pattern in place, and prick each numbered line with a nail or awl. (I have circled the holes in the photo).

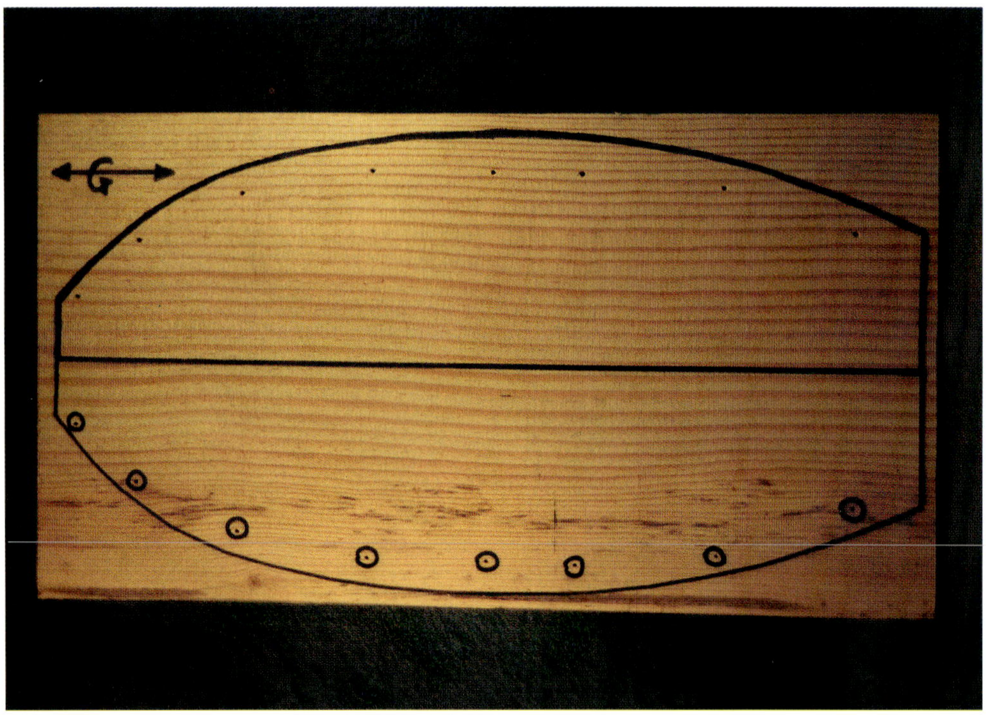

Now, flip the pattern over and prick the numbered lines again. (I have circled the holes on this half of the wood).

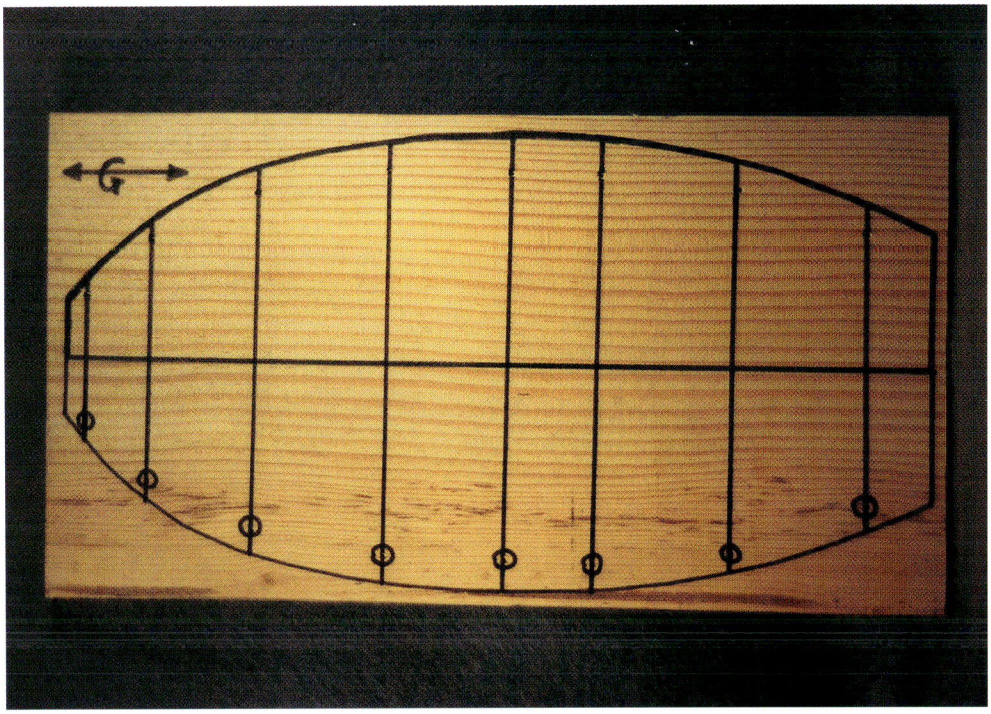

Use a straight-edge to connect the dots from one side of the pattern to the other. These will provide the reference lines we will need shortly to establish drilling holes around the edge of the bottom section. (Notice that we established a centerline running the length of the body, when the two pattern halves were traced to make a complete bottom section).

Using a bandsaw or jig saw, saw out the bottom section.

Measure 3/8" down from several of the reference lines you established, and put a light pencil dot there . (If you used 3/4" thick shelving, as I did, 3/8" is half of its thickness). Do this at several points all around the left and right edges of the bottom section.

Using the pencil dots as a guide, sketch a line all around the edge, until you have the thickness of the wood roughly divided in half. Don't panic if your line isn't exactly perfect all the way around. We're not building a moon rocket here, so just try to get it close to the center as you sketch your way around.

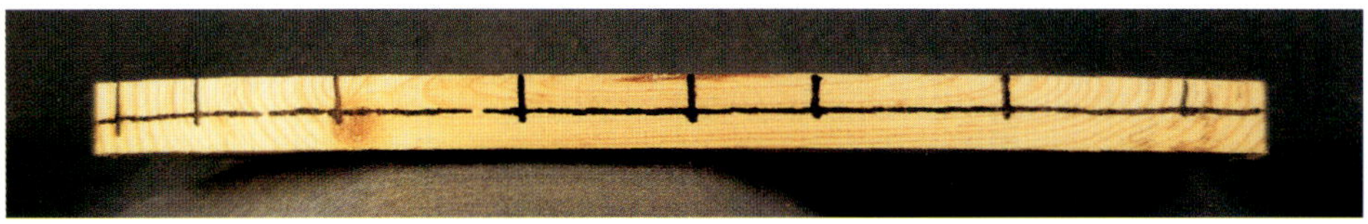

Now use the lines you drew across the top from one side to the other, and continue them down the sides until they intersect the line you just drew.

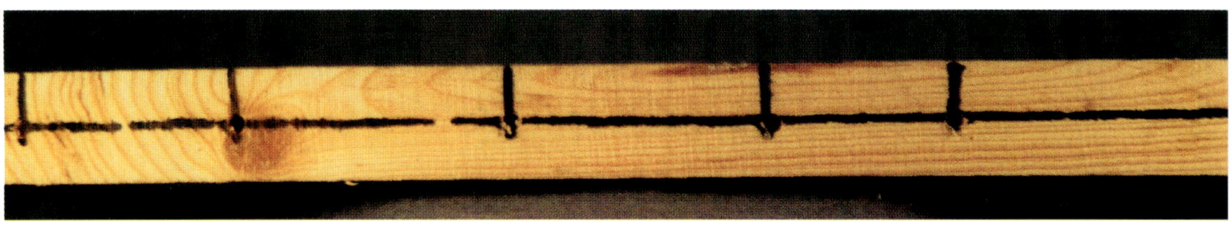

Next, drill a 1/8" hole about ½" deep straight into the edge (perpendicular to the edge), at each point where the lines intersected, all the way around. (Such as shown here). These will be the anchor holes for the wire hoops we will fashion in a later step. After drilling all the holes, set the bottom section aside. We'll come back to it later.

Now, transfer the pattern for the backbone section to an appropriate-sized section of 3/4"-thick shelving and saw it out. Pay attention to the grain direction so you will have maximum strength from the wood. Saw out the notched areas, also. These will help keep the wire hoops in place in a later step.

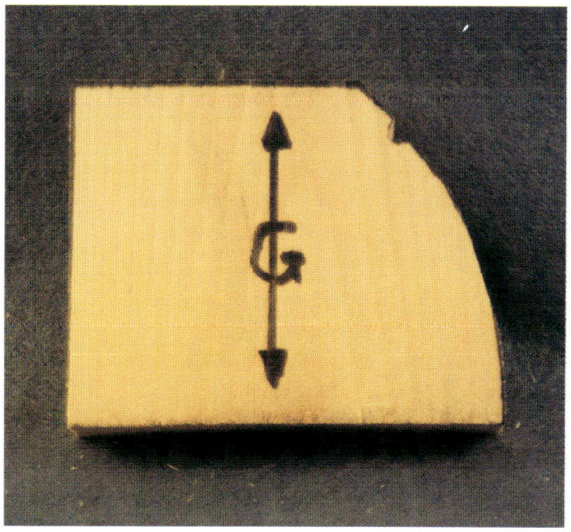

Transfer the neck (front) section pattern to an appropriate-sized piece of 2"x6" (nominal) wood, and saw it out. Saw out the notch, also. Observe the indicated grain direction.

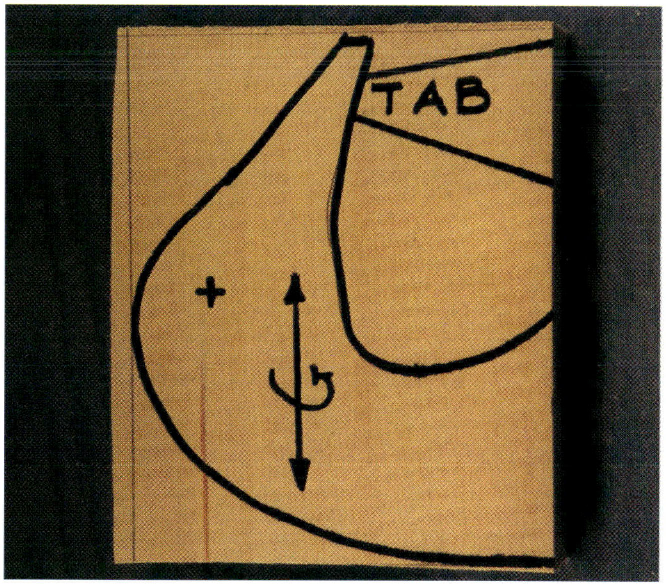

Transfer the head pattern to a piece of 1-3/4' or 2" thick basswood. Notice I have sketched in one of my famous "tabs" which will be used to help hold the head level in an upcoming step.

Mark the indicated location of the center of the eye with an awl or sharp nail. Then, drill a 5/16" hole all the way through the head section. Later, we will use 5/16"wood screw plugs to fashion eyes for our goose.

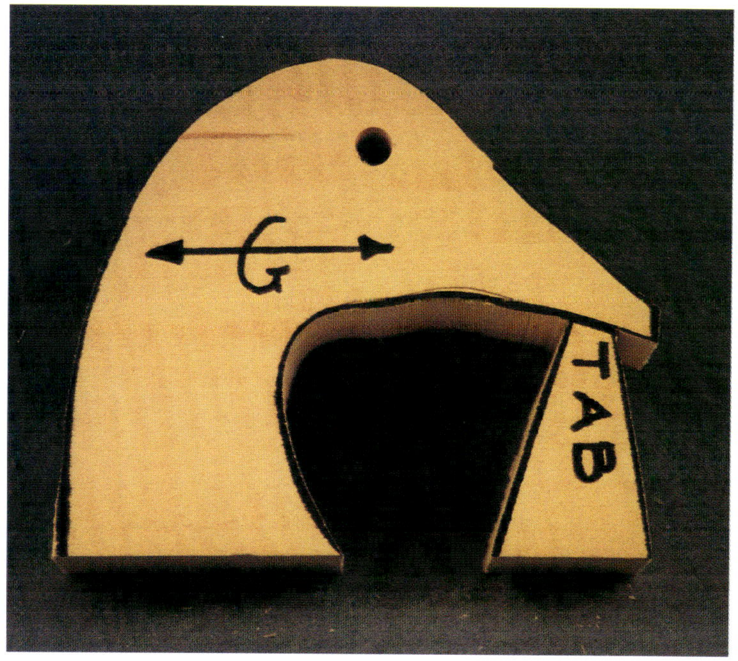

Now, saw out the side profile of the head, leaving the "tab" section in place for the moment.

Next, sketch in a centerline from the tip of the bill, up and over the top of the head...

and down the rear of the neck.

Now, saw out the top profile, following the lines you just sketched. (Here is where the "tab" helps hold the head level while you saw). Once the top profile is sawn out, you can *carefully* saw away the tab with your bandsaw, or you can use a coping saw or your knife to remove it. Use whatever method you are most comfortable with. Set the head aside for now, and we'll come back to it in a little while.

Sketch in the top profile of the bill and head, as shown here.

Set the backbone and neck sections in place, on top of the bottom section. Use the centerline you drew earlier to align the pieces from front to rear. Check for a good fit, and see that no wood protrudes from the front or rear of the bottom section. If necessary, mark any overhang. Re-sketch the wood, and use your saw to remove the excess now.

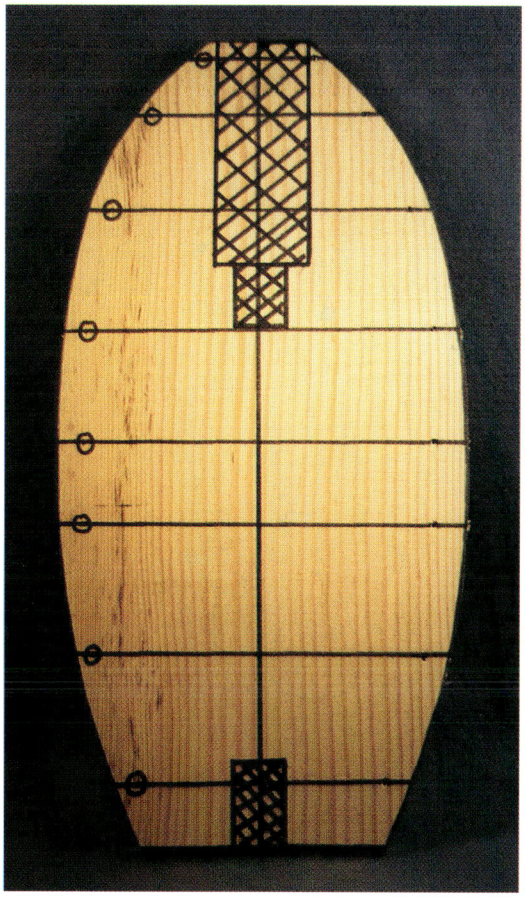

Above:
Turn the bottom section over, and counter-sink the holes so the drywall screws will fit flush with the bottom edge.

Above left:
When you are satisfied with the fit, put the two sections back in place. Lightly trace around them so you can see the areas that come into contact with the bottom section, once you remove the pieces. (Observe the cross-hatched areas in the photo).

Left:
Using a drill bit large enough for a drywall screw, drill holes through the bottom section as shown. Look at the dark circles in the photo, indicated by the arrows.

Place the neck section upside down in a vise, if possible, and secure it firmly.

Lay the bottom section in place over it (with countersunk hole facing up). Look underneath and use the outline you traced earlier to help line up the pieces.

Gently screw in a 1-1/2" drywall screw until it just starts to grab (go about 1/8" deep into the neck section). We are just making a reference hole at this time.

Now, loosen the screw enough to separate the two pieces, and remove the bottom section for a moment. Leave the neck section in the vise.

Apply wood glue to the part of the neck section that will come in contact with the bottom. Then, put the bottom section back in place. When it is aligned properly (check it with the guidelines you traced), tighten down the screw. The reference hole you made earlier will help guide the two pieces back together. Then, insert and tighten down the second screw in the neck section.

Repeat this procedure for the backbone section. Also, when you apply glue to the area of the backbone section that will contact the bottom section, put a thin line of glue on the front part of the backbone section (the area that will be butted up against the neck section). Set the completed assembly aside to dry while we work on the head.

At this point, here is how your assembly should look.

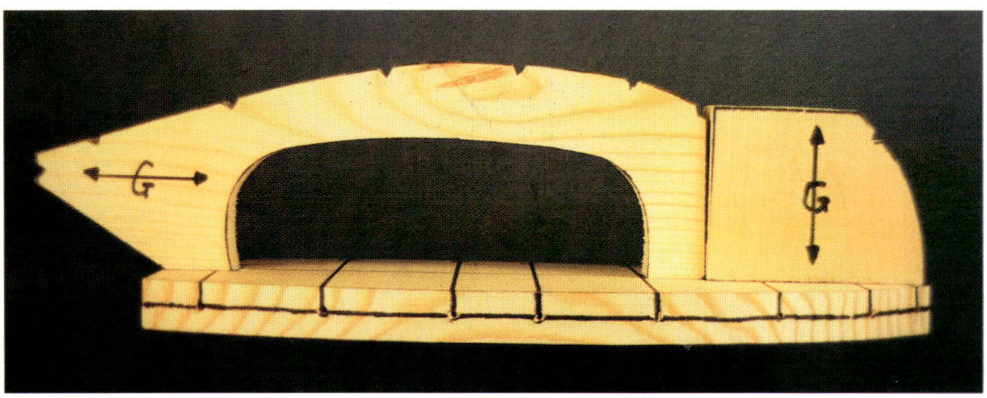

Now, attach the head to the "T"-Holding rig so it will be easier to carve and shape. (Here's where we'll start making the holding rig earn its keep). For work on the heads and necks, I use a smaller version of the "T"-holding rig.

Using your knife, remove the four sharp edges of the head so it assumes an octagonal shape. If you are more comfortable with a power grinder (rotary tool), use this to remove the sharp edges.

The head is not as square as it was, but it still needs more roundness. Using the same method as in the previous step, remove the new sharp edges. If you still want more roundness, remove the new sharp edges again. As you can see, this is an iterative process. The more times you remove sharp edges (on any carving), the more round it becomes. I am going to stop at this point, because I want to preserve some of the knife cuts and facets. I want the head to look "carved", not like it came from a plastic mold.

Round off the front edge of the bill with your knife, as seen in this top view.

You can probably see the taper better in this front view.

Now, using your knife or 3/4" (19 mm) straight gouge, remove some wood from both sides of the head. Start just below the eye holes, and remove more wood as you work toward the top of the head. This will form a taper from the eyes to the top of the head.

Carry the angle of the taper out to the end of the bill, so the bill will have a slight taper on the sides, slanting in from the bottom edge toward the top.

Sketch a line to indicate the separation of the bill from the head. Do this on both sides...

on top...

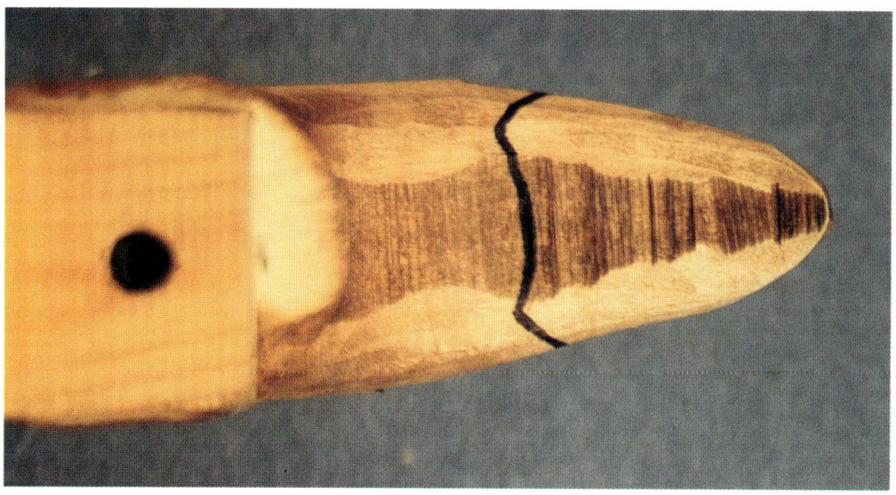

and under the bill. Remember, we are making a decorative decoy, so you have some flexibility as to the accuracy of the lines.

Incise these lines about 1/8" deep, all the way around, with the tip of your knife. Then, working *from* the head, *toward* the bill, shave away a small amount of wood so the bill will be separated and defined from the head.

For a little bit of extra detail, sketch a line on both sides of the bill to define the separation of the upper bill from the lower section.

Using your knife, incise the lines about 1/8" deep. Now remove these triangular-shaped pieces on the lower part of the bill using your knife.

At this point, look over the entire head. If there are still any marks remaining from the bandsaw, gently remove them with your knife to remove any extreme rough areas from the surfaces.

Now, insert a 5/16" rounded wood plug into each eye hole, and *gently* tap them in, until only a slight curve of the plug protrudes. More experienced carvers may want to use glass eyes and fashion eyelids from epoxy putty, but for this project the wood plugs are the least frustrating, and are the most economical.

Apply a small amount of wood glue to the bottom of the neck, and to the top of the neck section of the base. Rub this into the wood to "butter" the surfaces. After the glue has had about 5 minutes to dry, apply some fresh glue to the bottom of the neck and set the head into position on top of the neck section. Let this assembly dry overnight.

After the glue dried overnight, I decided to add just a bit more detail to the bill area. I used an **18mm, #7 sweep "U"-gouge** to scoop down from the head toward the tip of the bill. This removed a little more wood from the upper surfaces of the bill as seen here...

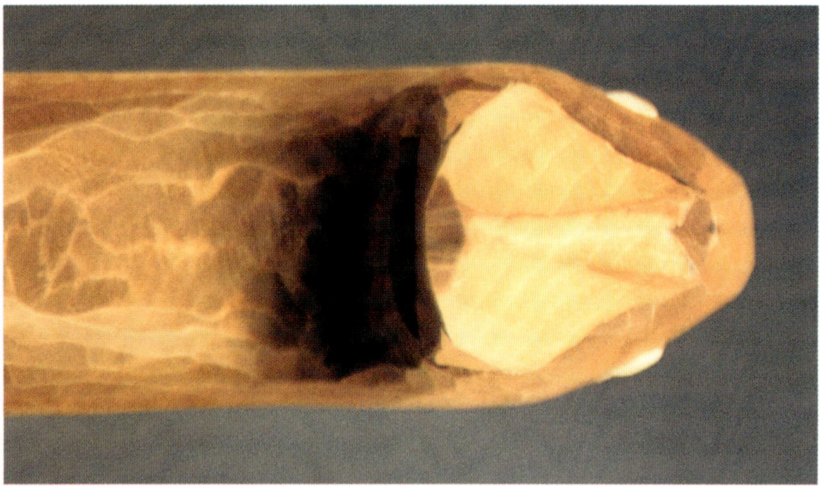

...and in this front view.

Attach the "T"-Holding rig firmly to the bottom section using the drywall screws. Then clamp the 2 x 4 vertical section firmly in a vise (similar to what is depicted in the photo), so we can get started with the wire hoops and canvas covering.

Partially unwind a section of #12 (12 gauge) steel wire which you can obtain at any hardware or building supply store, and insert it fully into one of the holes in the bottom section as shown here. Pull the wire over the back section, laying it into its appropriate notch, and hold it against the corresponding hole on the opposite side of the bottom section from where you started. *Observe the numbers shown on the pattern for the bottom section, back section and neck section to keep the notches referenced to their proper hole in the bottom section.* (Pull the wire as tight as you can, and observe where it intersects the hole. Mark this point with a pencil or permanent marker, then cut the wire about ½" longer than the mark you just made).

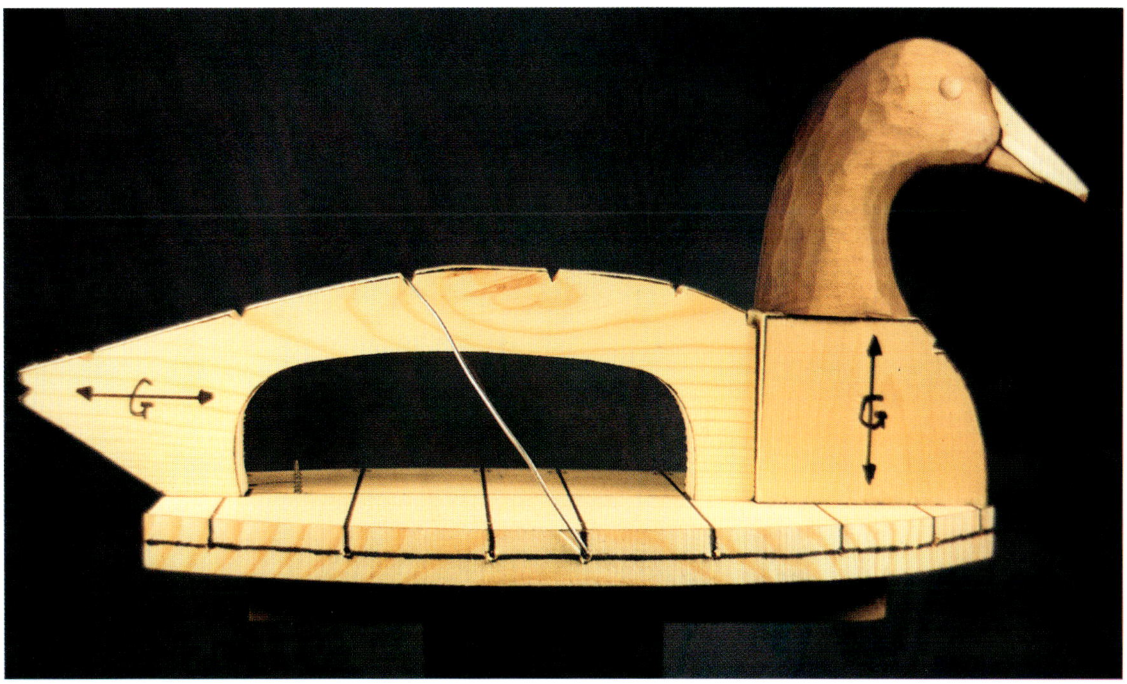

With pliers, bend this last ½" of wire inward 90° and insert it into the hole. There is a bit of trial and error in this step, and you may have to adjust the bend in the wire a little more or a bit less to get a good fit when you insert it into the hole. The effect you are striving for is a nice "hoop", similar to the ribs on the old covered wagons. If your hoop looks anything like this one, you are in business.

Repeat this procedure for all the holes and notches. At this time, your decoy should look something like this.

To further strengthen the hoops, and help hold them in position, you can use cotton twine such as I have done here, and run "stringers" from the front to the rear. Two or three stringers along each side is usually sufficient.

Covering the Body

Because I am making a decorative decoy, rather than a real working decoy, I am going to use unbleached muslin rather than canvas for my covering. This can be obtained at any fabric store. Since it is relatively inexpensive, I normally purchase several yards at a time. You can even use an old bed-sheet or cotton shirt, as everything is going to be hidden by paint eventually.

Drape a section of the muslin over the framework. You want enough material on the sides and rear to reach all the way around and under the bottom. Once you have the width approximated, add about a foot to the length to allow enough material to fit around the neck and under the front of the body. Using scissors, cut this entire rectangle free from the rest of your muslin.

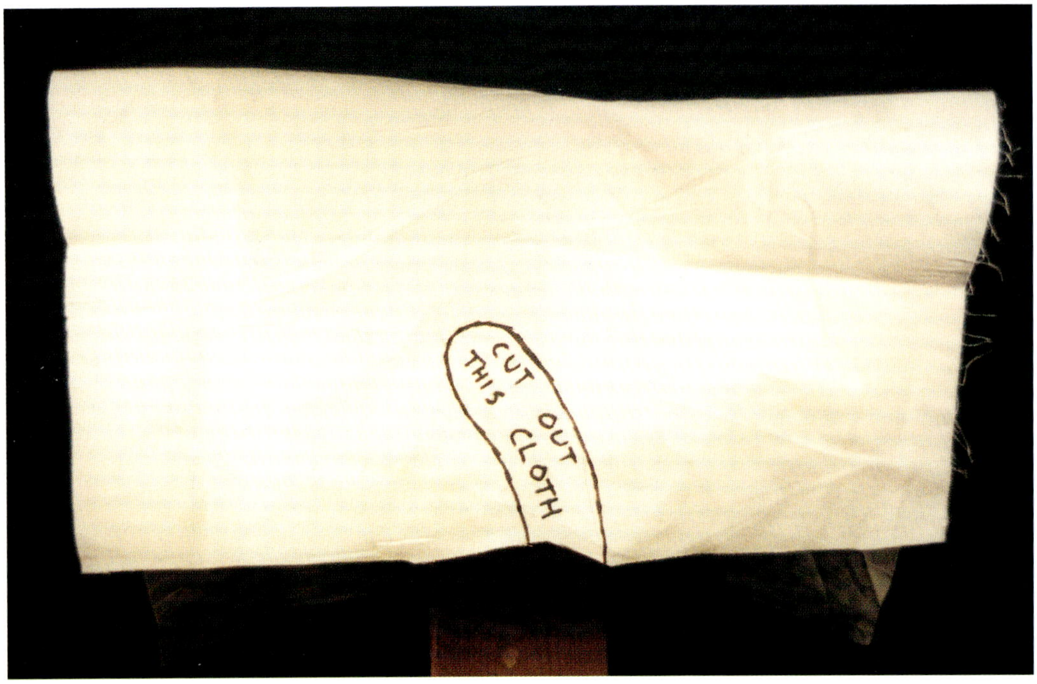

In the front section (approximately in the center) of the rectangle, cut out a slot about 1-1/2" inches wide. The slot should resemble a banana half, and should be rounded at the rear so it will better fit around the neck. It should be long enough to allow the cloth to reach under the bottom in front, when pulled taut.

Using small carpet tacks or a staple gun, fasten the cloth to the neck. Work from the front around to the back...

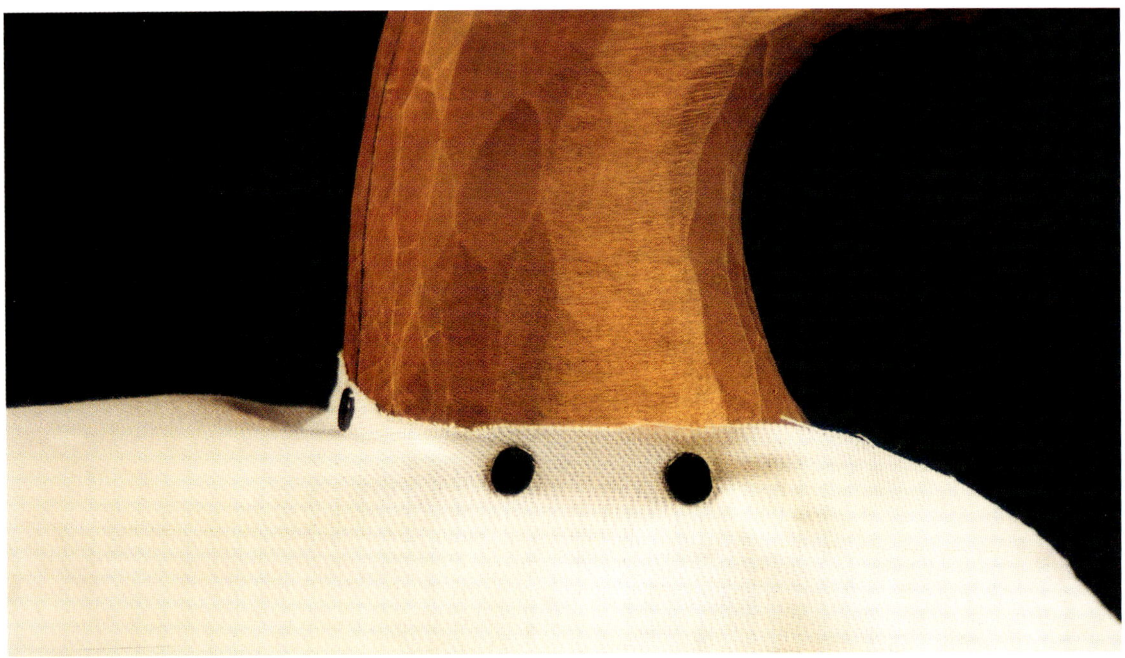

and back around to the front again.

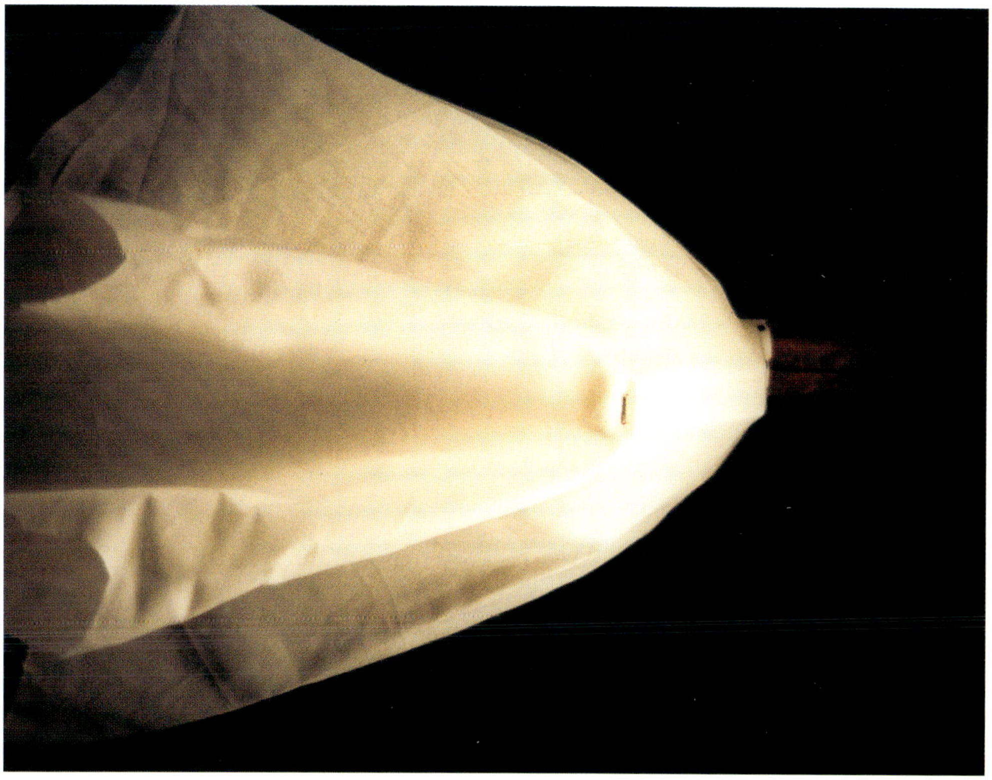

Next, pull the cloth taut over the back section, from front to rear, and tack or staple it to the rear of the tail, as seen here.

Pull one of the flaps down the front of the neck section and under the bottom, keeping tension on the cloth so it will fit tightly against the wood. While holding the cloth taut, use a staple gun or a tack, to temporarily fasten the flap to the bottom of the body as shown here.

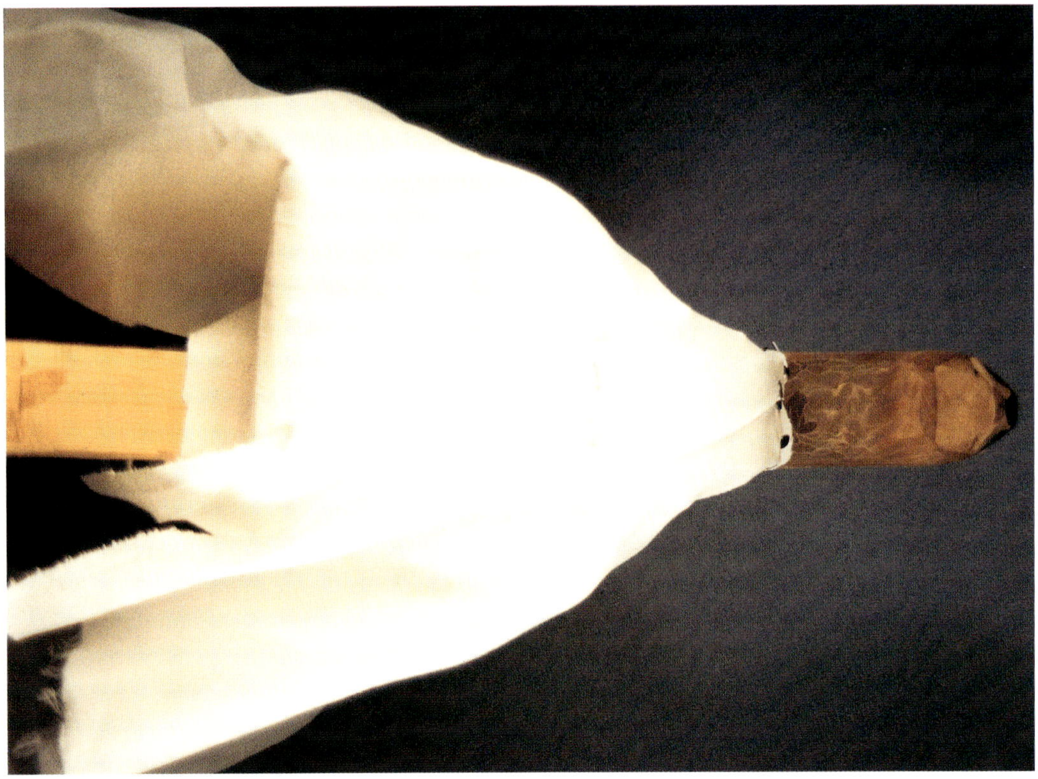

Repeat this procedure for the other flap.

Now, working from the front toward the rear, pull the cloth down the sides and under the bottom. Do one side, then the other. As you pull it under the bottom, use a staple gun to temporarily tack it in place. Continue this process until you get to the rear of the body.

At this point, you should have everything but the tail covered, and the cloth should be fairly tight all the way back. Pull one section of cloth tight against the rear edge of the tail section, and staple it in place along the rear...

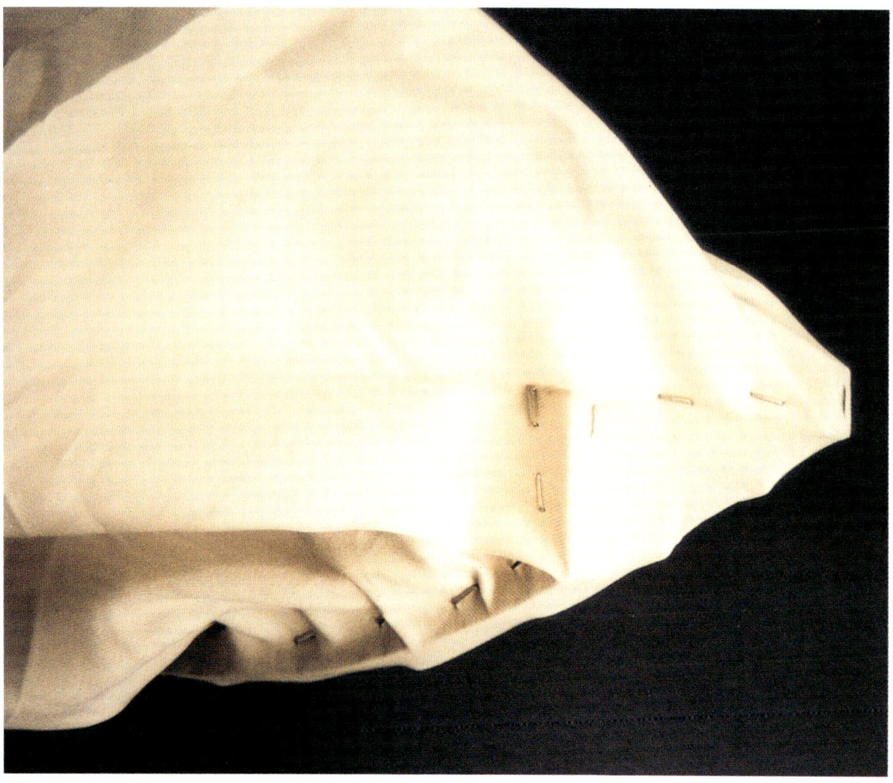

and under the bottom.

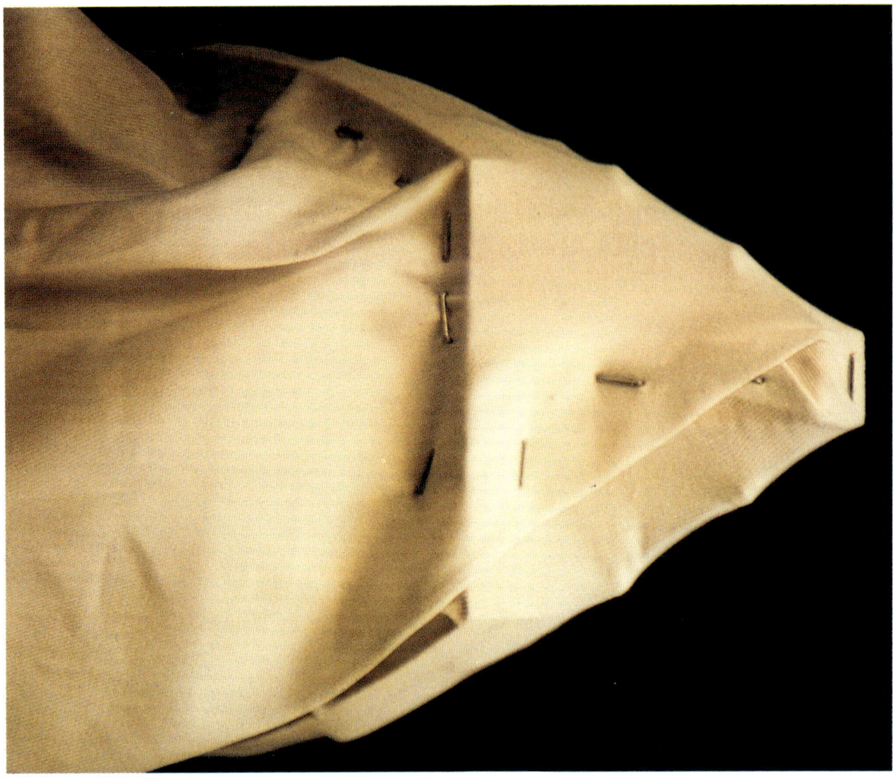

Cut away most of the excess cloth bunched up at the rear. You want to leave just enough material to finish covering the rear of the body, without having an abundance of wrinkles. Staple this last flap in place along the rear edge, and also under the bottom.

To finish off the body, before we trim away all the excess material on the bottom, you will need some 1" wide rug-binding tape, folded in half to a double thickness (it looks similar to one of the web belts used by the military, but is much softer). You can obtain this in hobby stores or other stores where rug-making supplies are sold. If you can't get this, take some of the muslin and fold it to a double ½-inch width. Start at the rear of the tail, and tack a strip in place all the way down the rear edge. Trim it even with the bottom.

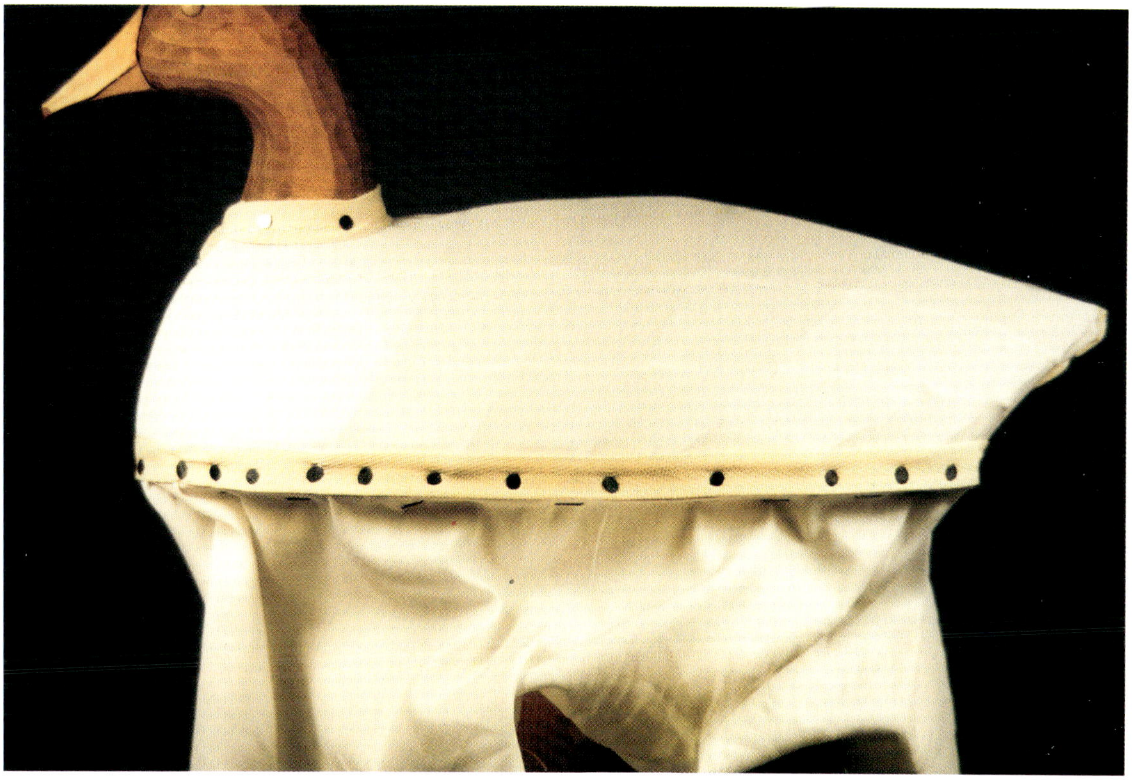

Now, starting at the rear, tack another strip of cloth or rug tape all the way around the bottom edge, until you end up in the rear once more. This keeps the majority of the seams at one end of the decoy.

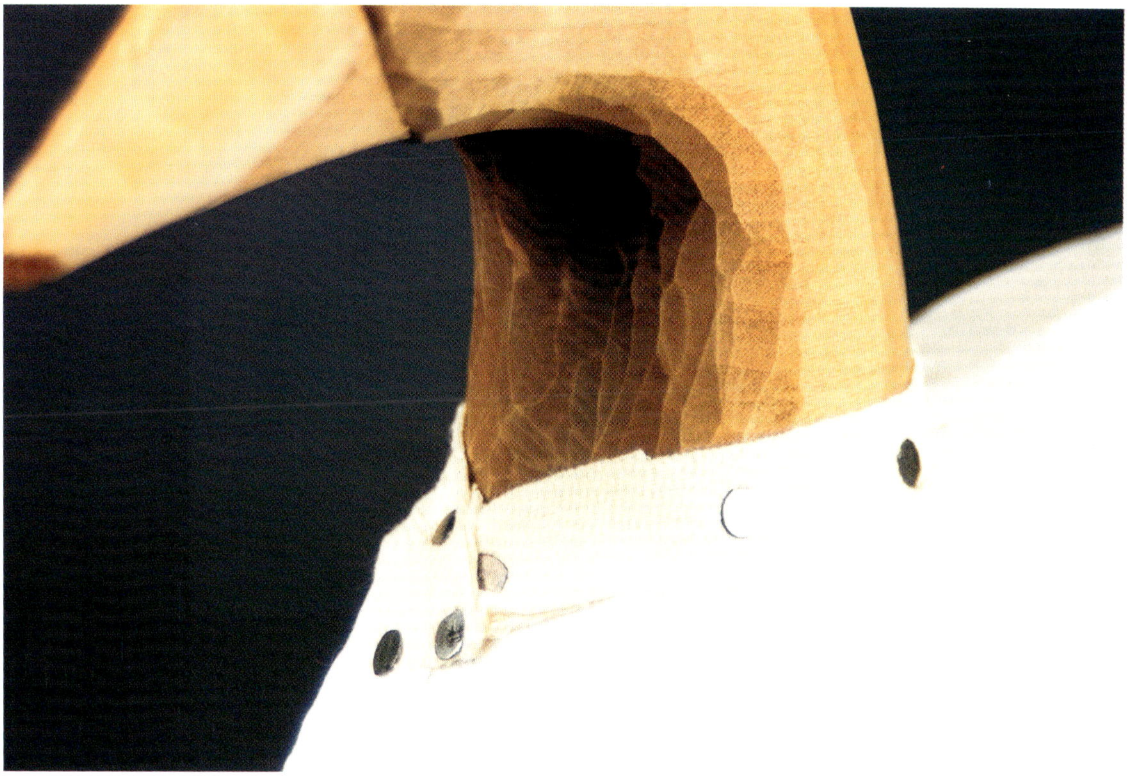

I also put a strip around the neck, to cover up the raw edges of the muslin.

Finally, remove all the staples or tacks from the bottom of the body, and trim away all the cloth even with the bottom edge. A sharp knife or single-edge razor blade works wonders here.

Painting the Goose

Prime the entire goose with white gesso or flat white latex paint. Let it dry overnight. This will stiffen the cloth, and will tighten up the cloth even more as the primer dries. I let this white primer show through in the areas that are to remain white when the painting is completed (the antiquing will soften it and tone it down).

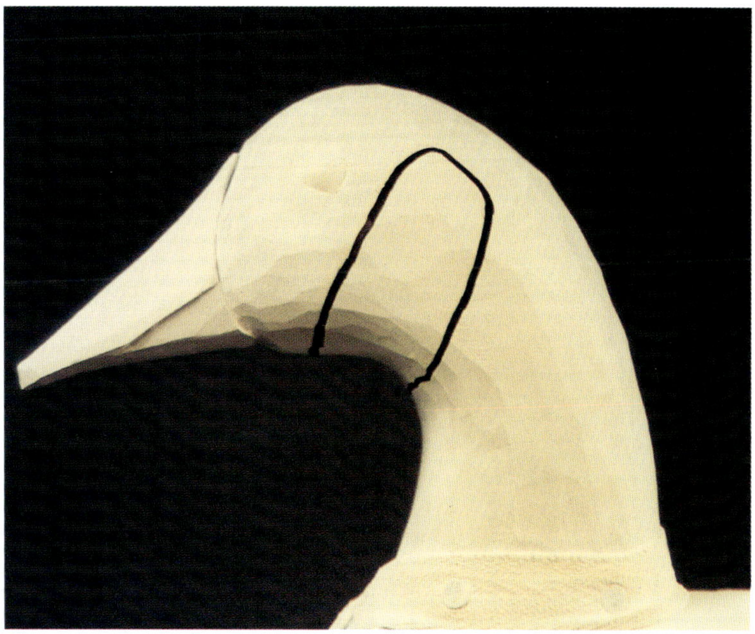

Sketch in the lines for the neck patch...this patch goes down one side of the head, under the neck, and up the other side of the head.

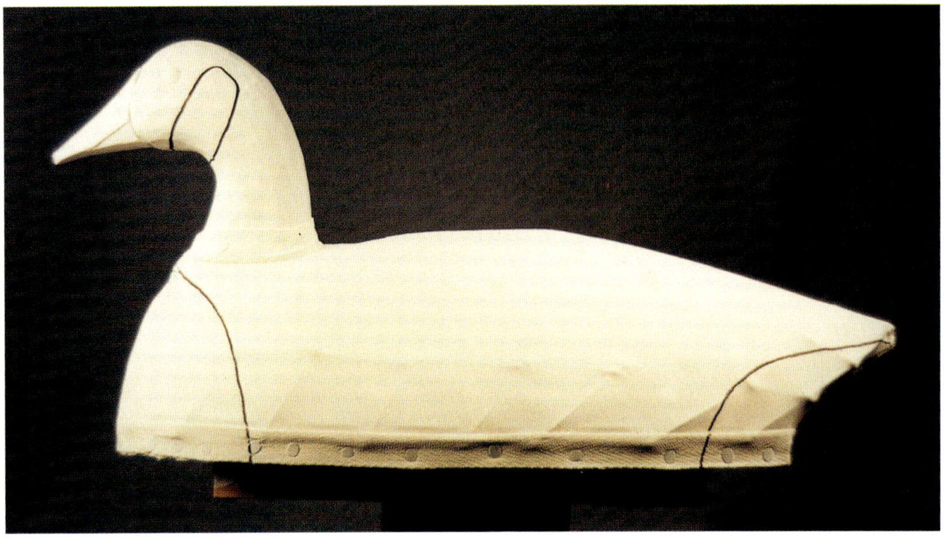

Next, sketch in the lines to define the color separations on the body.

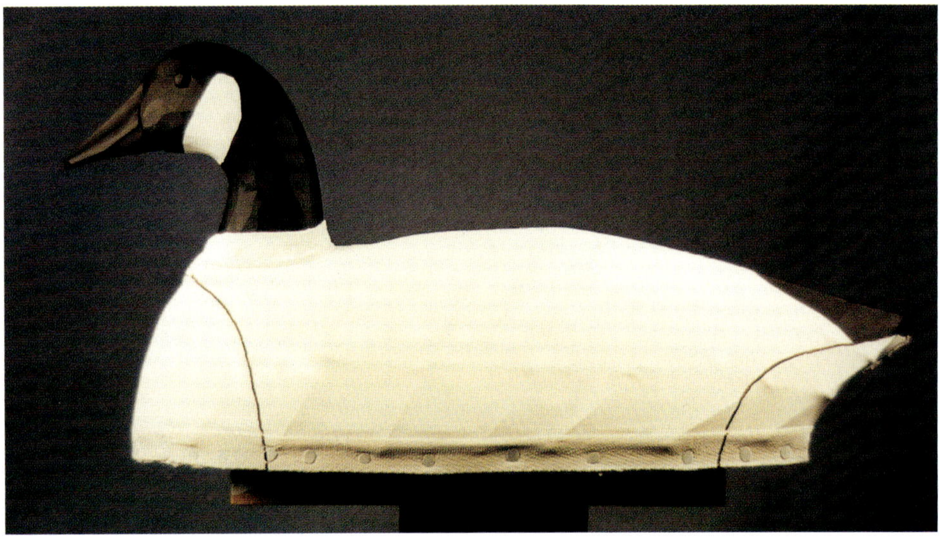

The head and tail patch are painted black—notice I left the neck patch white. I painted in the tail patch free-hand. If you are not comfortable doing this, sketch in some guidelines first.

The main part of the body is painted Territorial Beige, while the front and rear remain white.

Antiquing the Goose

If you wish to "age" your decoy, you can do so by applying an antiquing solution to the entire goose, then wiping it off with an old towel or soft rag. The longer you let it remain on the goose before you wipe it off, the darker the final outcome will be. (It is an acrylic solution, so don't let it dry completely, or you won't be able to remove it). Delta makes a variety of antiquing colors, so you can look at them in the store and determine which color(s) appeal to you. For aging decoys, I would suggest using solutions with brown tones, rather than the ones with red or green tones.

I am not applying any varnish to the finished project. Our project is made to resemble a "working" decoy, and birds in real life are not shiny or glossy. By applying antiquing to the decoy, we are giving it the effect of many years of faithful use out in the elements.

Side view of completed project, after antiquing.

Front view of completed project.

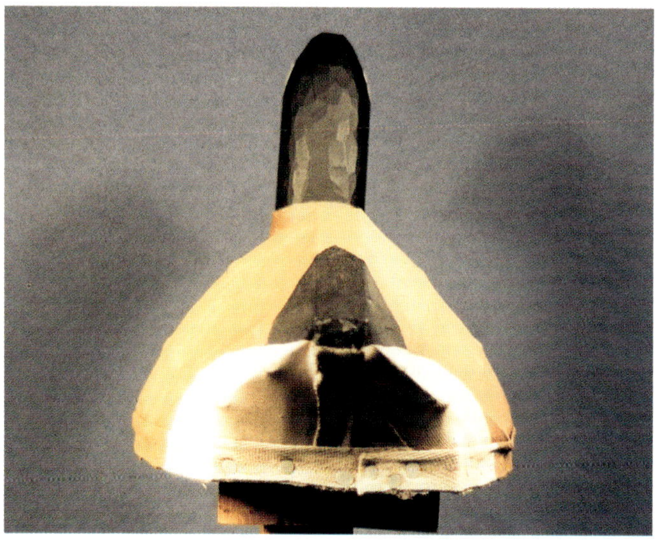

Rear view of completed project.

Top view of completed project.

In order to help "immortalize" your decoy, sign your name on the bottom, and include the date. If you don't already do so, you should also number the work. As you become famous in the years to come, collectors will seek the items you made which have low numbers on them. These will indicate prize pieces from your formative years, when you were developing and perfecting your own, unique style. As a general rule of thumb, collectors don't like to acquire pieces which are not signed, numbered and dated.

I hope that in some way I have been able to help each of you with some aspect of carving and painting. When we share tips and information, we all become better. If you have any comments or questions about something in this book, or if you have an idea you'd like to see me put in a future book, please feel free to write or call me at the following address and telephone number. I welcome any comments or suggestions you have.

Al Streetman
402 North Broad Street
Guthrie, OK 73044
(405) 282-8234

THE GALLERY

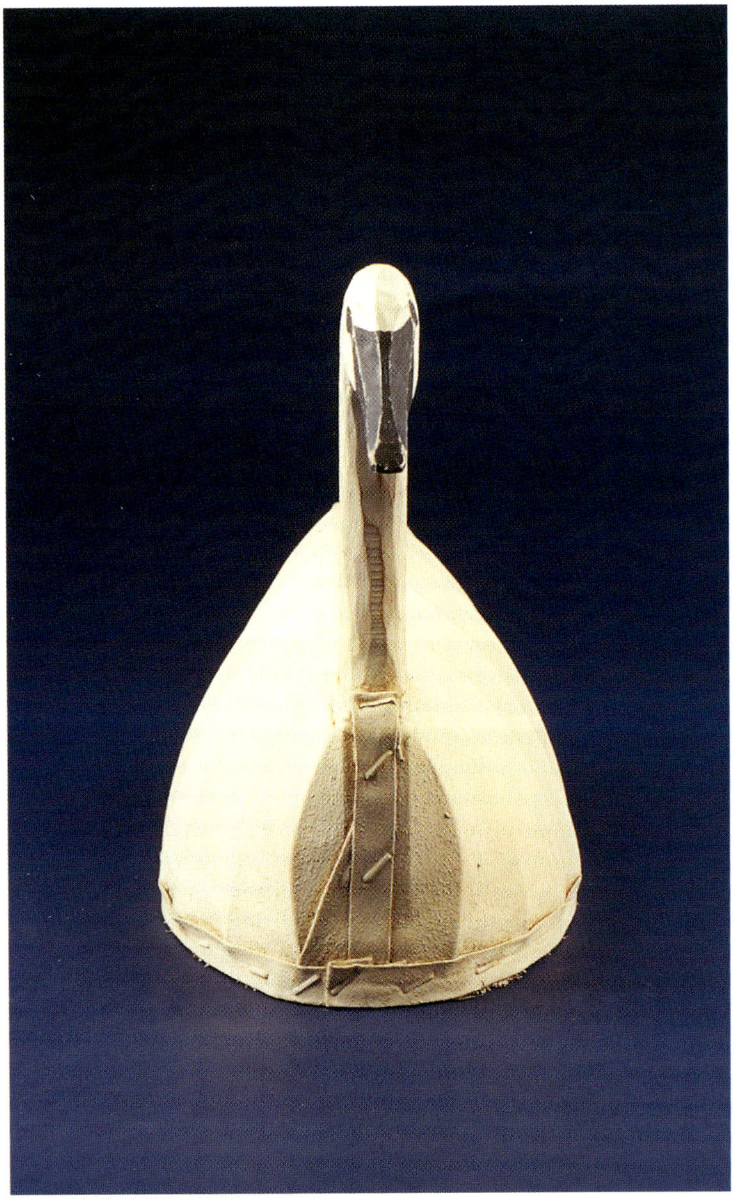

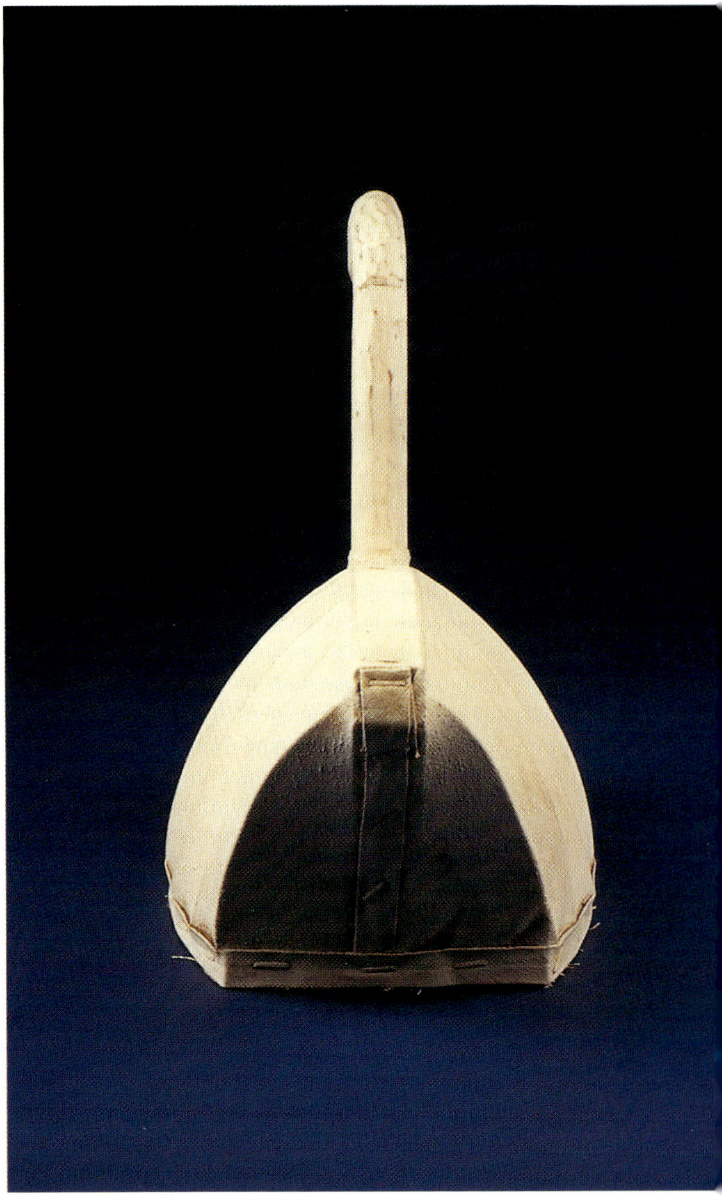

"T"-Holding Rig for working on decoys:

Top section: 1"x4"x9" (nominal): Nail and glue this piece to the top of the 2x4 for extra strength.

Bottom section: 2"x4"x12" (nominal).

Use two wood or drywall screws inserted through holes drilled in the top piece. Screw them firmly into the bottom of the decoy.

These will hold the decoy securely while you work on it.

You may wish to make several rigs, in different sizes, to accommodate various sizes of decoy bodies.

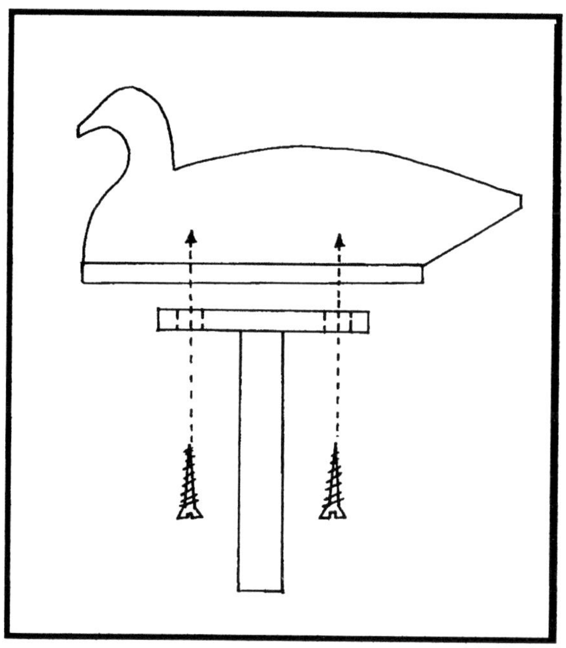

Gouge Reference Chart

General Woodcarving Gouges

Square Chisel

Inch	mm
3/8	10

Skew Chisels

Inch	mm
1/8	3
3/8	10

Straight Gouges

Inch	mm
1/4	6
1/2	13
3/4	19
1/8	3
1/4	6
3/8	10
1/2	13
3/16	5
3/8	10
1/8	3
3/8	10
3/4	19

Veiners

Inch	mm
1/8	3
1/16	1.5
1/4	6

Bent Gouges

Inch	mm
3/4	19
3/8	10

Spoon Bit Gouges

Inch	mm
3/8	10
3/8	10

V Tools

Inch	mm
1/8	3
1/4	6

Micro Carving Gouges

Blade Size

Square Chisel
5mm

Skew Chisel
4mm

Dog Leg Chisel
5mm

Straight Gouges
2mm
3mm
4mm
5mm
5mm

Bent Gouges
3mm
5mm

Veiner
2.5mm

V Parting Tool
3mm

Reprinted with the permission of Robert Sorby

Sources of Supplies

Woodcrafters of Oklahoma
116 S.E. 74th
Oklahoma City, Ok. 73149
1-888-333-7513(Ask for catalog)
High-quality tools and supplies.
New items constantly being added to their line.

Robert Sorby
Athol Road
Sheffield S8 OPA, England
Superior hand tools, carving knives, and gouges.

Wood Carvers Supply, Inc.
P.O. Box 7500
Englewood, Florida 34295
1-800-284-6229 (Ask for catalog)

Smoky Mountain Woodcarvers Supply, Inc.
P.O. Box 82
Townsend, Tn. 37882
1-800-541-5994(Ask for catalog)

Little Mountain Supply, Inc.
179 Bowling Green Road
Front Royal, Va. 22630
1-800-752-7573(Ask for catalog)

Craftwoods
P.O. Box 527
Timonium, Md. 21094-0527
1-800-468-7070 (Ask for catalog)

Delta Technical Coatings, Inc.
2550 Pellissier Place
Whittier, Ca. 90601
1-800-423-4135 (Ask for catalog)
Excellent acrylic paints and finishes.

Royal Brush Mfg., Inc.
6707 Broadway
Merrillville, In. 46410
1-800-247-2211 (ask for a catalog)
Quality, affordable paintbrushes.

DecoArt
P.O. Box 386
Stanford, Ky 40484
1-800-477-8478 (Ask for catalog)
Excellent acrylic paints and finishes.

WoodCraft Bands, Inc.
6159 Hwy 421
N. Vilas, NC 28692
828-297-6081 (Ask for catalog)
Quality Bandsaw and Scrollsaw blades, with a large savings in price per blade.

Mountain Woodcarvers
150 East Riverside
P.O. Box 3485
Estes Park, Colorado 80517-3485
1-800-292-6788 (Ask for catalog)

General Reference and Information Sheet
(for all the patterns in this book)

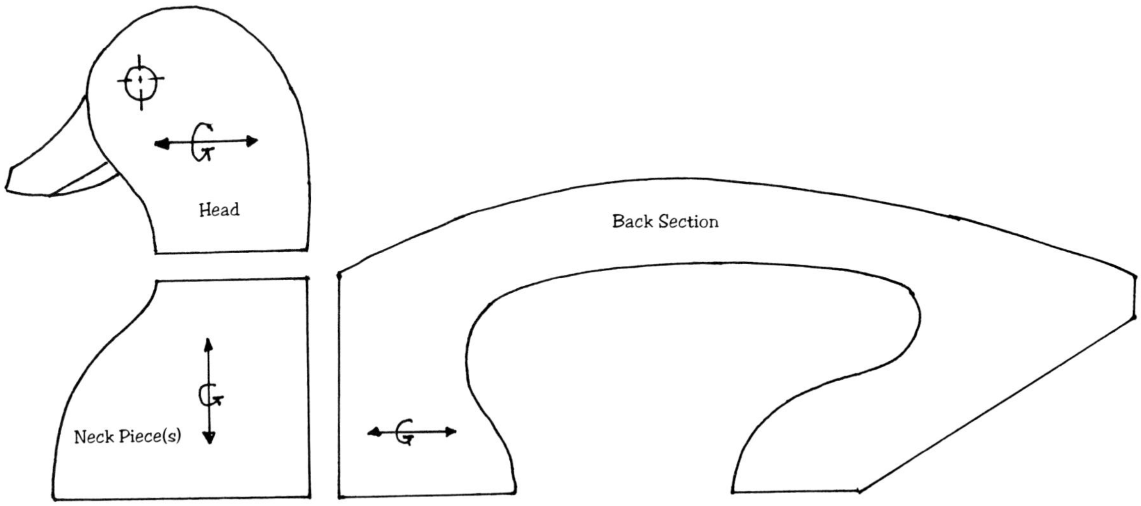

Arrows, with "G" superimposed over them, indicate recommended direction of grain for maximum strength.

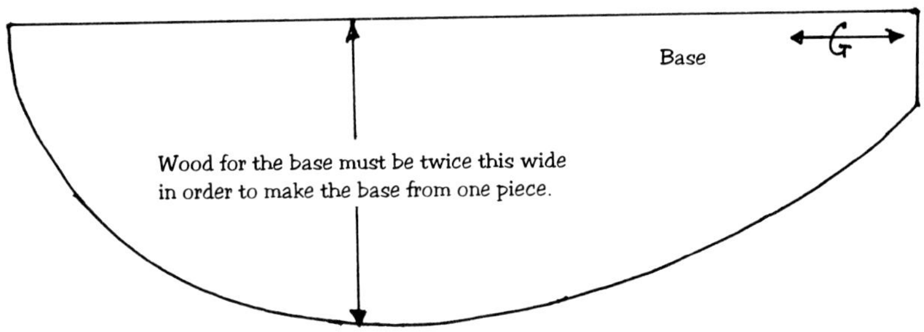

<u>Suggested Materials:</u>
(Nominal wood sizes)

Head: Basswood, 2" thick

Neck Piece(s): Pine, 2"x4"; 2"x6", or other width as required by the pattern.

Back Section: Pine Shelving, 1"x6"; 1'x8", or other width as required by the pattern.

Base: Pine Shelving, 1"x6"; 1"x8", or other width as required by pattern. (Remember... only <u>half</u> of the width of the base is shown on the pattern!!)

Eyes: 1/4", 5/16" or other diameter wood plugs as indicated by the pattern. (More advanced decoy makers may want to use glass eyes....it's your choice.)

Enlarge at 166%
for full size

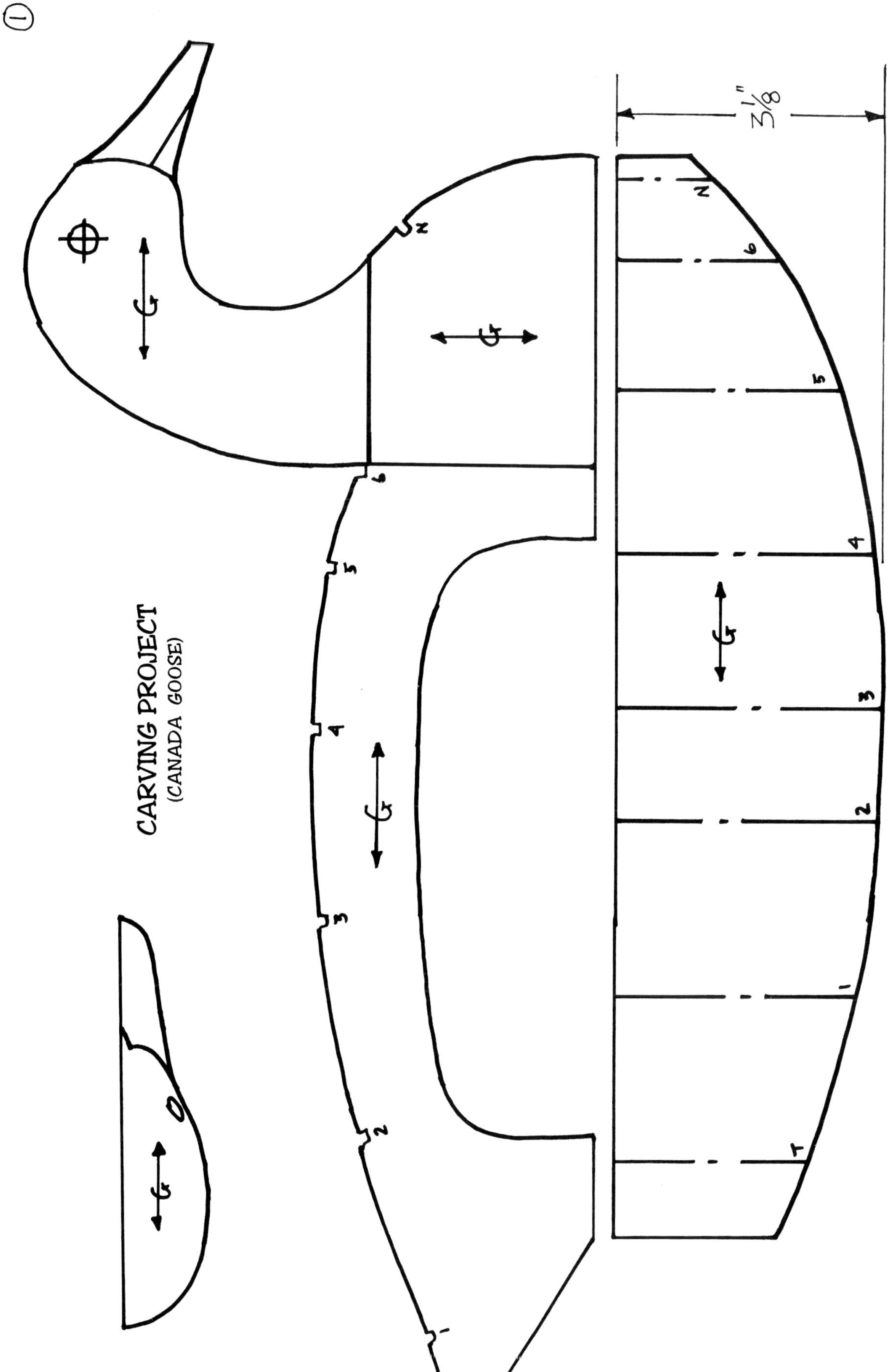

Enlarge at 166%
for full size

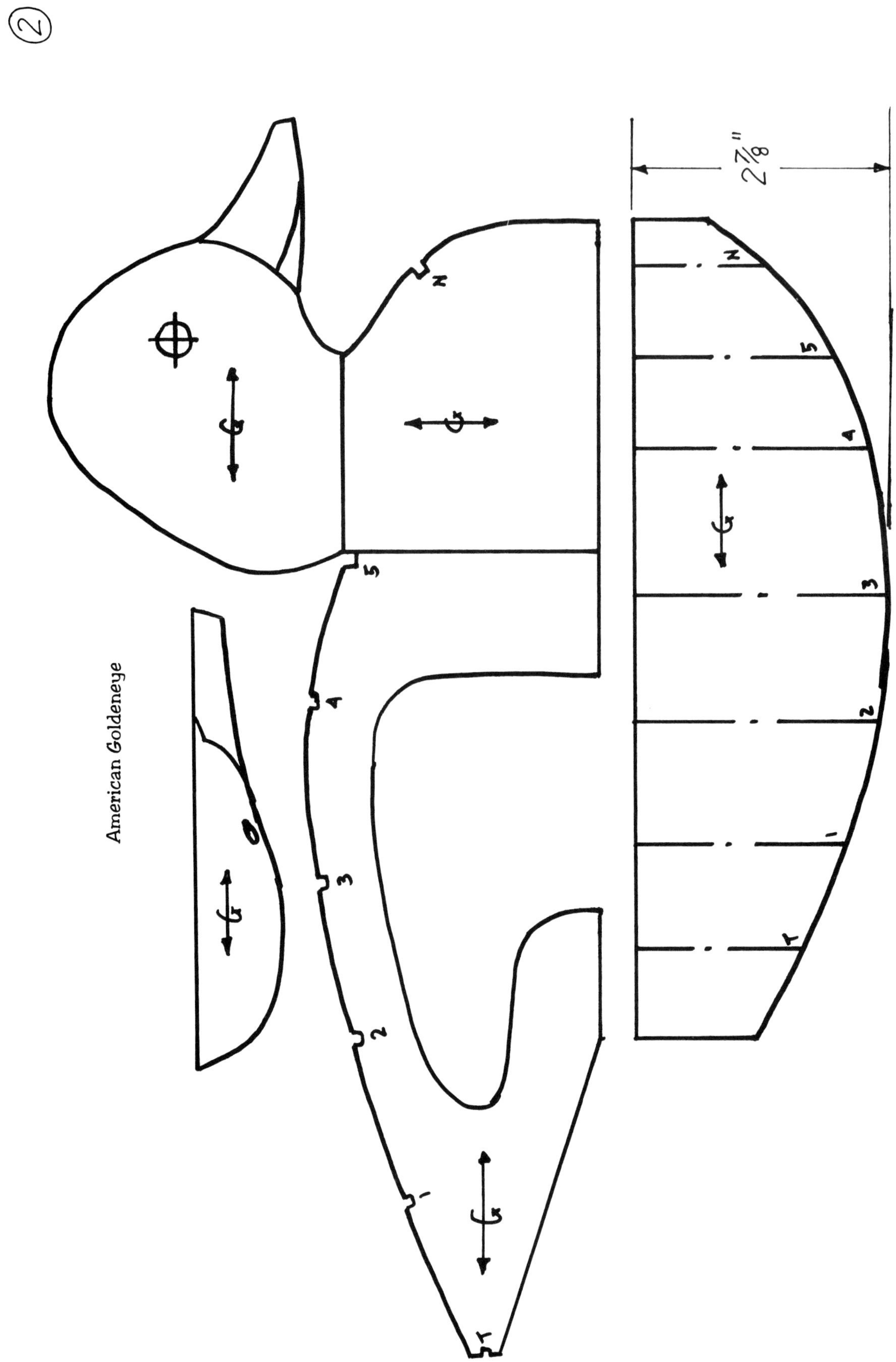

Enlarge at 166%
for full size

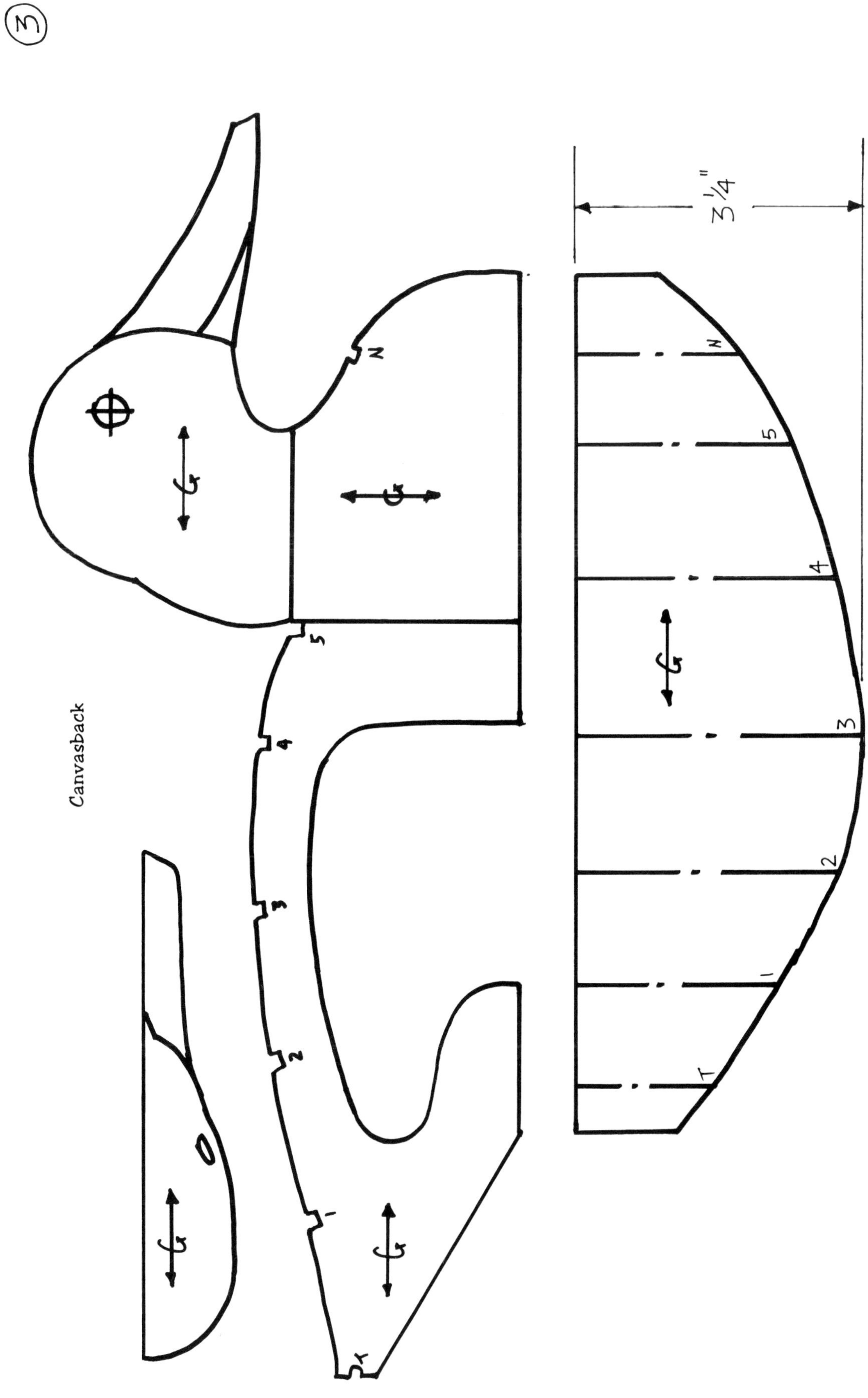

Enlarge at 166%
for full size

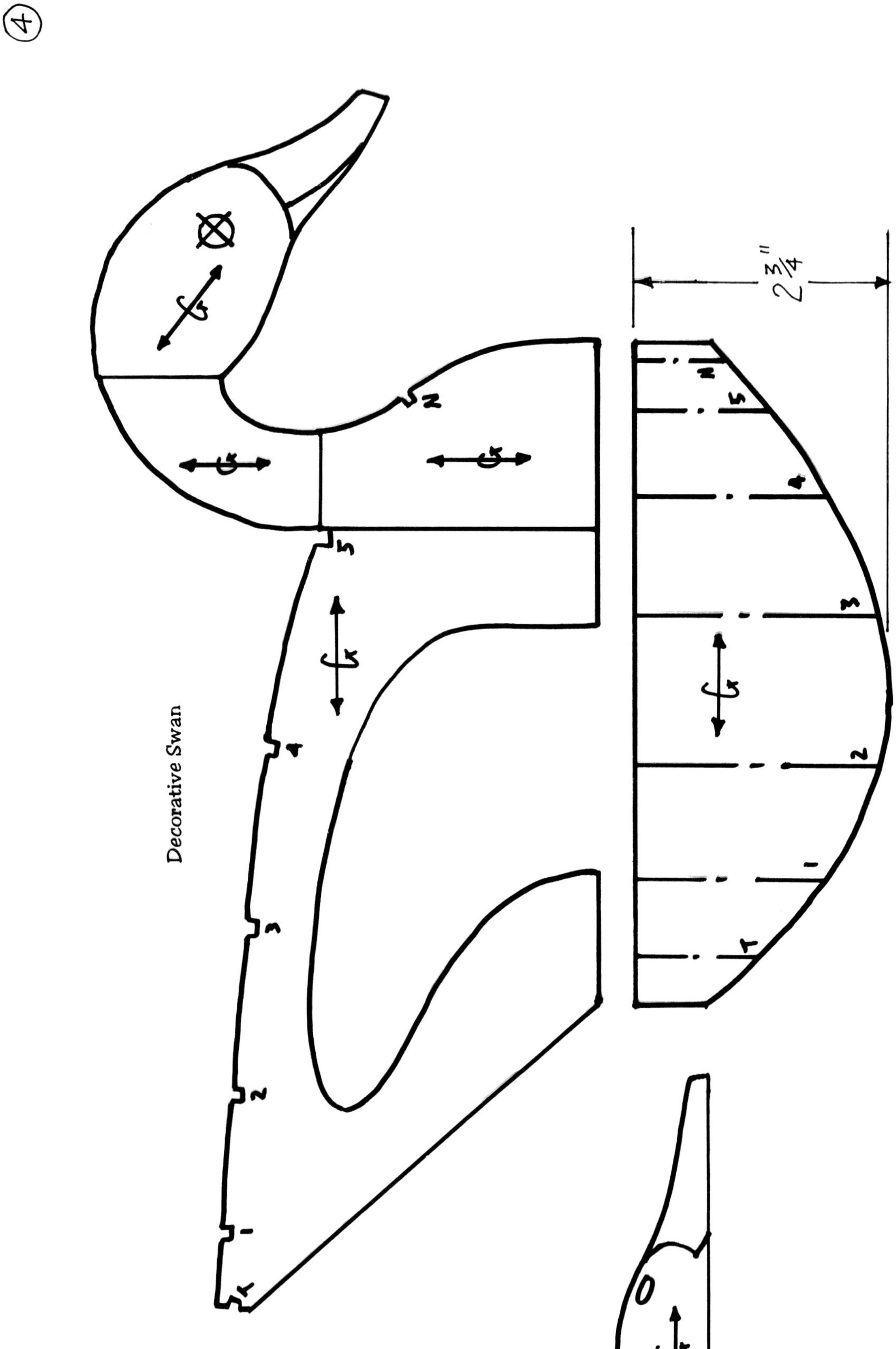

Decorative Swan

Enlarge at 166%
for full size

(5)

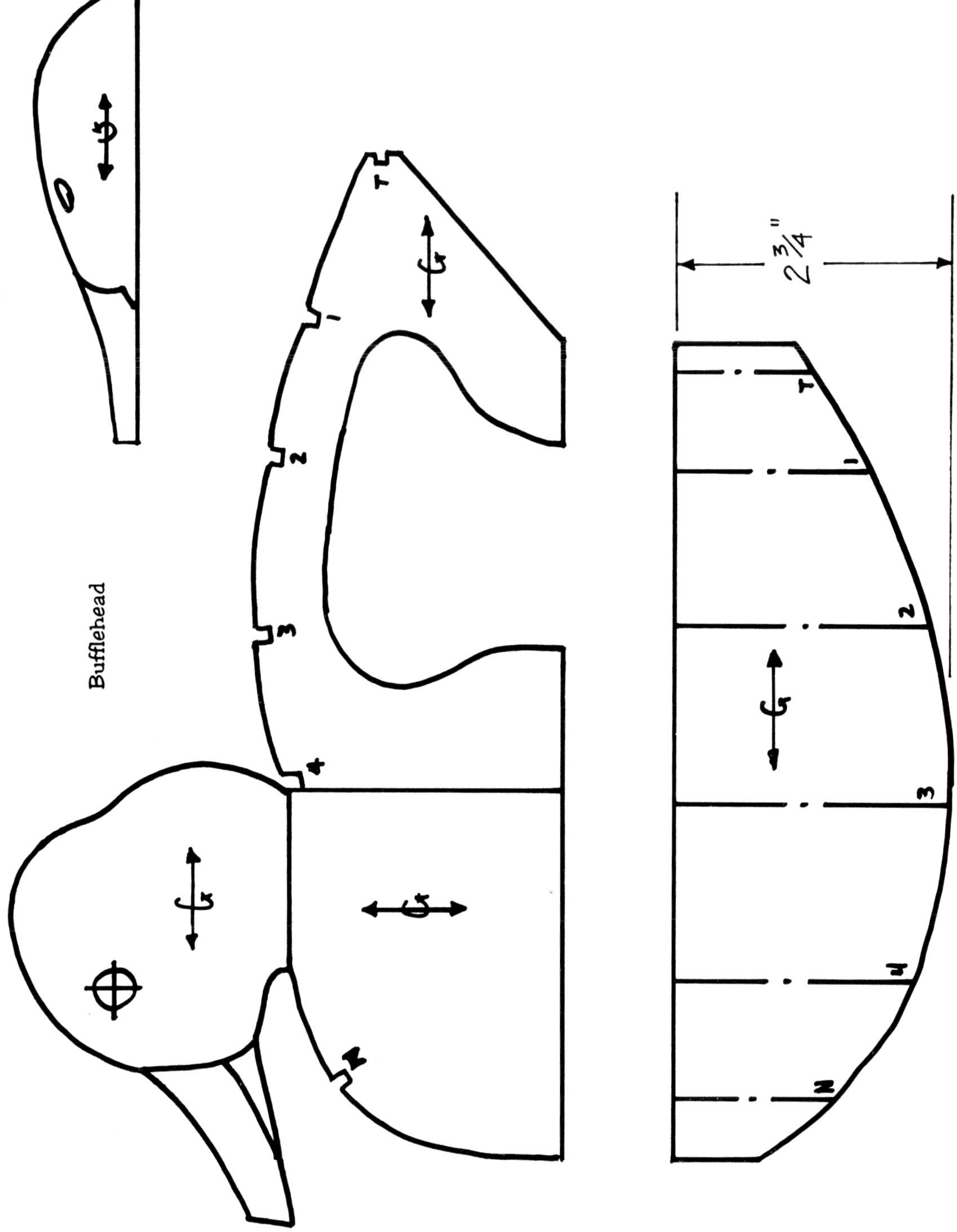

Enlarge at 166%
for full size

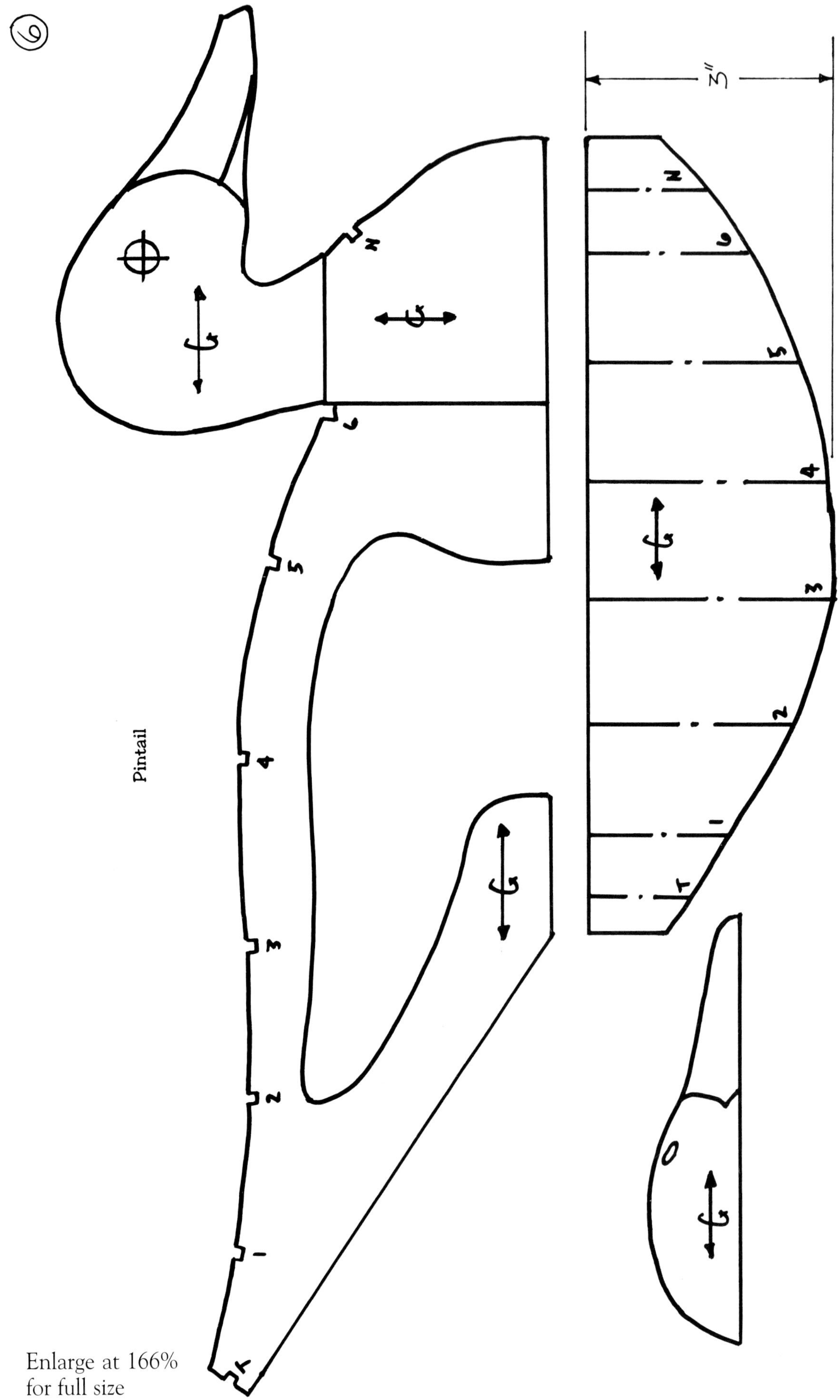

Enlarge at 166%
for full size

7A

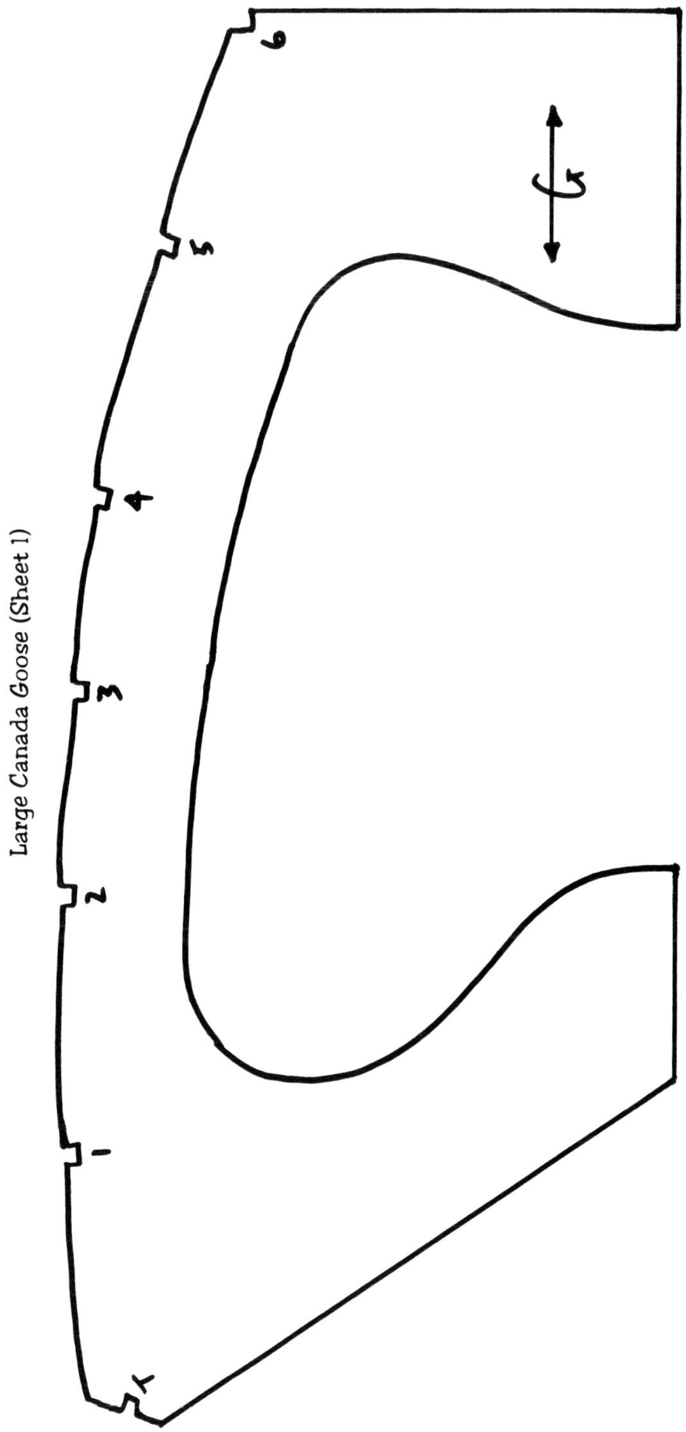

Enlarge at 166%
for full size

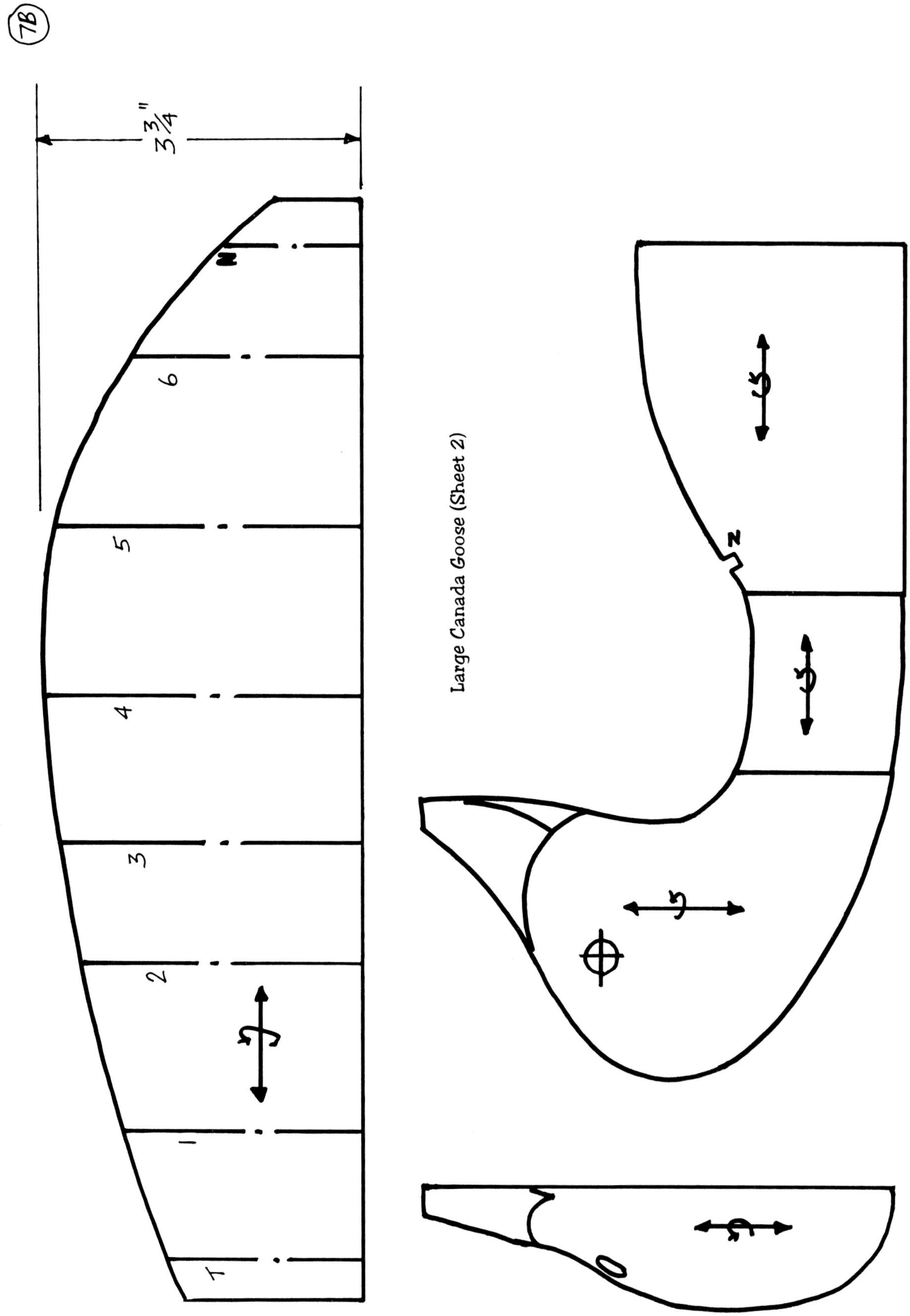

Large Canada Goose (Sheet 2)

Enlarge at 166%
for full size

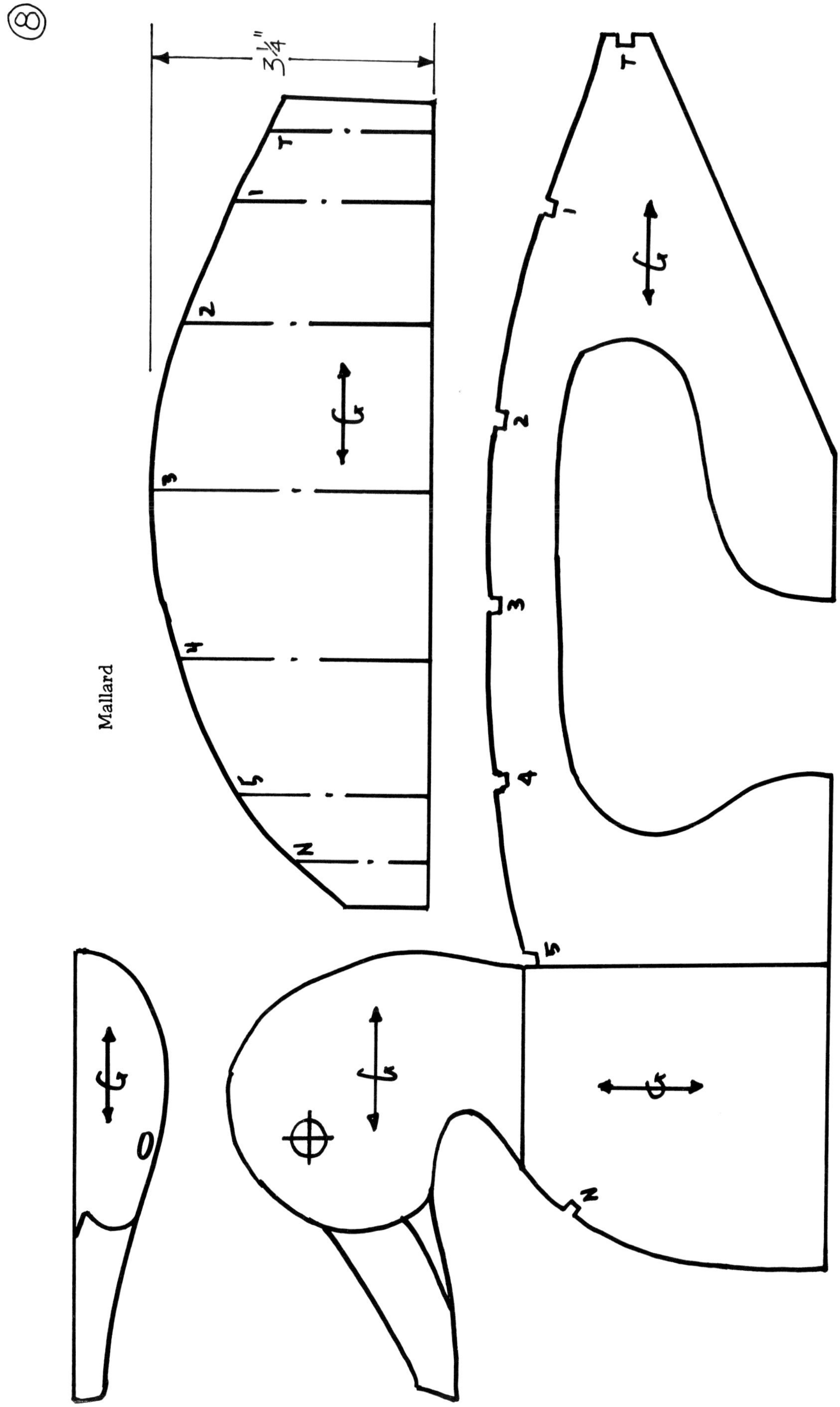

Enlarge at 166%
for full size

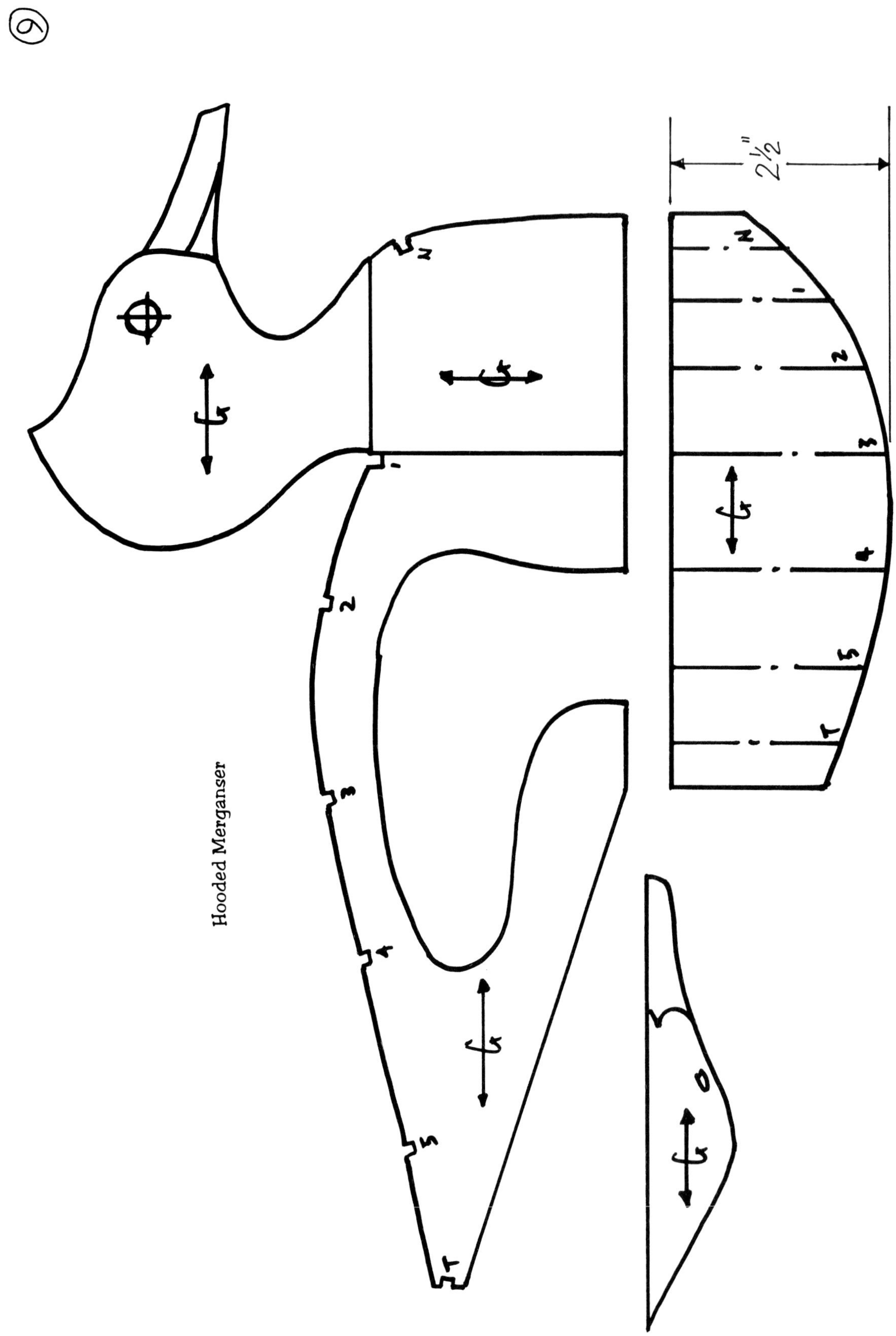

Hooded Merganser

Enlarge at 166%
for full size

10

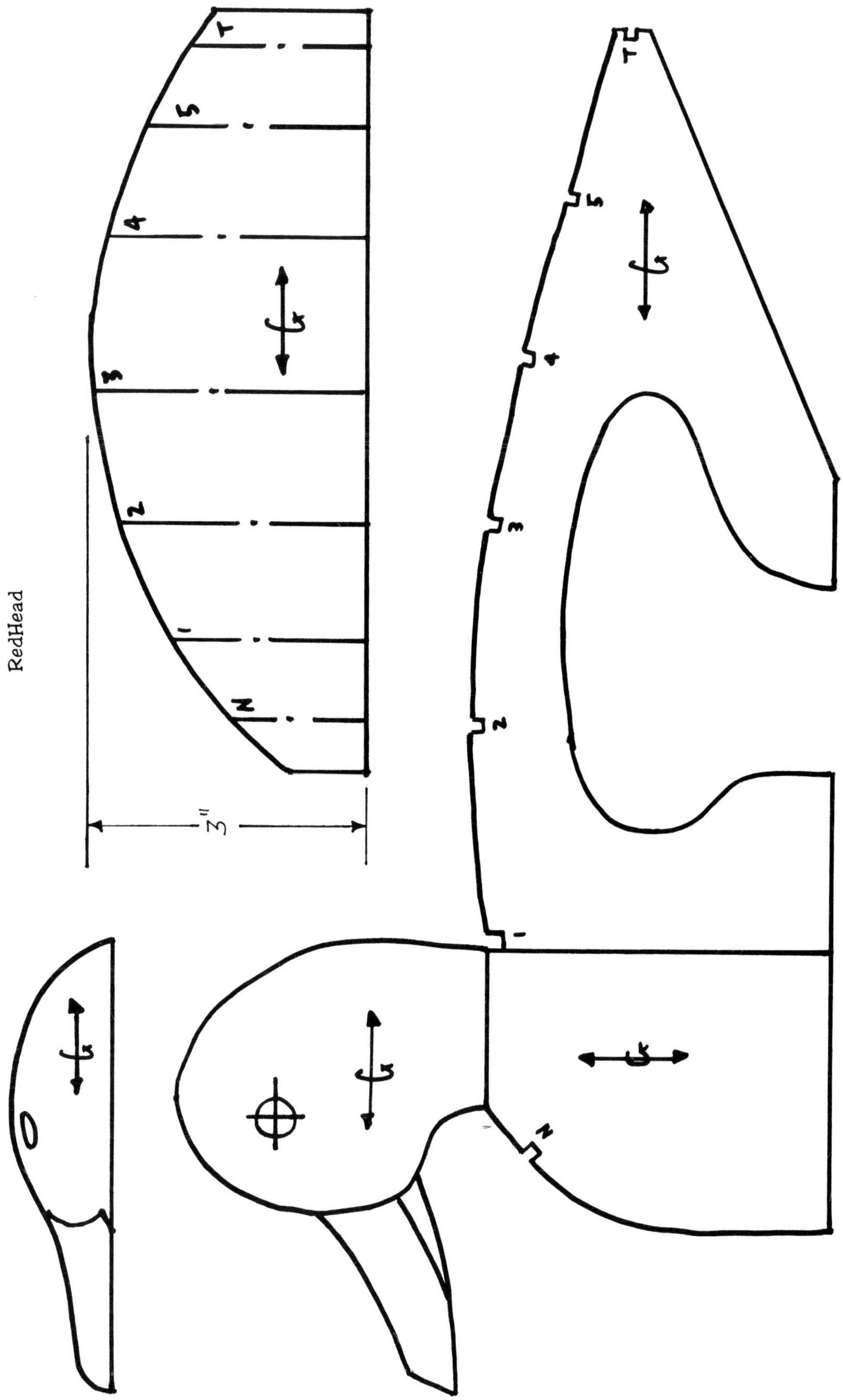

Enlarge at 166%
for full size